MW01274741

Think
and
Thank

**Getting from where you are
to where you want to be**

JOHNBOSCO U. OZURUOME

 FriesenPress

One Printers Way
Altona, MB R0G 0B0
Canada

www.friesenpress.com

Copyright © 2024 by Johnbosco U. Ozuruome
First Edition — 2024

All rights reserved.

ISBN
978-1-03-830926-6 (Hardcover)
978-1-03-830925-9 (Paperback)
978-1-03-830927-3 (eBook)

1. SELF-HELP, MOTIVATIONAL & INSPIRATIONAL

Distributed to the trade by The Ingram Book Company

Table of Contents

Preface   vii

Foreword   ix

Introduction   1

PART ONE: JUST THINK   5

   Chapter One: Stop Worrying, Start Thinking   7

   Chapter Two: Know Your DCA   37

   Chapter Three: If You Don't Have it, Search for it   61

   Chapter Four: Knock the "T" Off Can't   79

PART TWO: JUST PLAN   95

   Chapter Five: Stop Thinking, Start Planning   97

   Chapter Six: To Live in the Present Day   115

   Chapter Seven: Doing The Same Thing,
Receiving the Same Result   129

   Chapter Eight: Across The Bridge   141

PART THREE: ACTION PLEASE!   155

   Chapter Nine: Stop Planning, Take Action   157

   Chapter Ten: Don't Lock Horns, Lock Hands   167

   Chapter Eleven: You've Got Lemons, Make Lemonade   175

   Chapter Twelve: Success Tomorrow is
Today's Preparatory Action   181

Bibliography   185

Index   189

Acknowledgments   201

About the Author   203

Preface

Some time ago, during my undergraduate studies in science and the arts in Nigeria, a group of students gathered together in a round-table discussion. These students were content but were not satisfied with who they were and what they had. They wanted to make society a better place to live, while observing that the world is still an imperfect and unfinished product of the Creator. They were students who had soared and are still soaring with eagles, not chuckling with turkeys. The one distinguishing factor amongst these people was their mindset – how they perceived things. They saw gold where the rest merely saw iron.

They were people who were on a journey to find out why the world works the way it does – why things are the way they appear to be. From a philosophical perspective, these people were trying to understand the fundamental nature of things rather than their accidental attributes. It would not be wrong to call them ambitious people of principles and realistic. Thus, as a result of their research and brainstorming around making society a conducive place to live, this book came to be written.

Dear reader of *Think and Thank*: this book is for ambitious people. It is solely for you who want to get ahead faster. The ideas of the "founders" of this book have been distilled down in the pages ahead and will (I believe) save you years of hard work in achieving your desired goals. There are many things this book can do for you, including:

- Help you move away from the camp of mediocrity.
- Help you not settle for less than you intend to have and achieve in life.
- Help you achieve your goals faster than you thought possible.

- Teach you the psychology of writing down your goals, which I call DCA (Definite Chief Aim).
- Help you change your thinking patterns and thoughts.

And much more!

The biggest waste of time and life is for you to spend years accomplishing something that you could have achieved in only a few months. By following the techniques outlined in this book, you will be able to accomplish much more, in a shorter period of time, than you have imagined before.

By following these simple and easy-to-apply methods and techniques, you can move quickly from rags to riches in the weeks, months, and years ahead. You can transform your experience (just like I did) from poverty and frustration to satisfaction. Simply, you will succeed more than you ever thought possible. Allow people to observe the real you and experience a new life. You are about to take on a new and prosperous adventure – welcome it.

Happy reading!

Johnbosco U. Ozuruome

Foreword

A Dreamer, an Achiever

It isn't a surprise. The author's invitation is like Napoleon Hill's recommendation from Andrew Carnegie back in 1908; an opportunity that would grant him access to 500 top achievers in business, politics, science, and religion in order to discover the common denominators for success. It was through that interview that one of the New York Times Best Seller books, *Think and Grow Rich,* was written and published. In the course of the first chapter, Hill tells a story of a man named R. U. Darby who gave up on his dreams of becoming rich by prospecting for gold – a mere three feet before a major gold vein was hit.

So also, this book. From the tête-à-tête with the author, the completion of this book came about the author's interaction with "people of success" and his research and searches eons of years ago. Getting him right; the sole intention for this novelty is to bring to limelight: the prime principles that savored great people over the ladder of success.

For some time now, I have been searching for a work of literature that could take me all round. Thus, in a nutshell, this book is an all-rounder – taking you, for instance, showcasing for you "how" and "why" you should put a stop-loss to your worries, having definite chief aim, pushing hard the hand of the clock (time management), and lots more. They're too numerous to count; best left for the reader to discover the "raw ore."

This is a book on success; although this concept has varieties of meaning. To Zig Ziglar and to Brian Tracy (American motivational speakers, and success trainers and consultants) this takes on different dimensions. In today's global landscape, we truly need to keep reminding ourselves that once we find our definite major purpose and create our mastermind, it's our responsibility to continue the quest, no matter how hard the challenge. Every one of us holds a gift that is meant to be shared with the world. The author shares his gift in this book

Leaving no stone unturned, the "big bang" here is that the author exposes to the general public that sometimes in our lives, opportunity is disguised as setbacks or difficulties. Amidst all these, that is when you should continue, for you may be just three feet from your pot of gold. Don't wait till everything is just right; for it may not be perfect.

Put succinctly, within the pages ahead, I invite you to discover your own pot of gold – your special gift. The write-up is practical! It's put down in an easy-to-read and easy-to-understand format. Remember that *success leaves clues*. The clues are inside – just some pages ahead of you. Don't stop until you have gone through the pages (with a pen and paper to make some notes). I recommend you use what you have learned here: for what is power if not the application of knowledge. You are like a teabag. Remember to **Think and Thank**. Happy reading and good luck!

Dr. Jude Osuchukwu, MD
Mother of Mercy Hospital, Orlu, Imo State, Nigeria

To my parents, Mr. Theophilus and Mrs. Eucharia Ozuruome, whose love and understanding in marriage I so much admire. This book is a by-product of my parents' love and care.

Introduction

"The journey of a thousand leagues begins with a single step."
—Confucius.

Think and Thank is a book about success. Of course, the definition of success is relative. The success I emphasize in *Think and Thank* is the progressive realization of the worthy ideal. The two key elements are "progressive" and "ideal." Notwithstanding the sphere of life in which you seek success, the achievement is never definite, for life itself is always changing.

Think and Thank will be a reference guide for you. It was written out of real-life experience and long years of thorough research. It is a hybrid of nonfiction and fictional ideas, and I have attempted to investigate why some people are "rich" and happy, while the majority are "poor" and unhappy. One of my astonishing findings was that while the majority of people worry, few people think. In other words, the ability to think (rather than worry) constitutes your level of attaining the worthy ideal in life.

Throughout this book, you will see me reference the Bible and Jesus Christ. I am a Christian, and I am fortunate (and also humbled) to be a believer. The book you're holding in your hand is not just a self-improvement book. Success is predictable. Thus, this is a book of timeless principles used by successful people throughout history, which I have observed and studied for many years. Most importantly, I have applied these principles to my own life. The phenomenal level of success I now enjoy is the result of applying them day in and day out since their discovery. I am now the author of several books, have conquered stage fright and mastered public speaking, have graduated from college programs, and have mastered the art of negotiation.

My own story and how I started

This is a wonderful time to be alive, and every effect has a cause. I was born in and grew up in the eastern part of Nigeria. My dad was a mechanic, and my mother was a trader who was skilled in buying and selling. One of the admirable qualities about my parents was how hardworking they were.

It was unconventional to "go the extra mile," but my conception about life changed when I entered college. I received the great bang when I encountered "a man of all trades," a friend in my undergraduate who was called Mr. Solomon ("Demore," as he was commonly called). Solomon was highly skilled, talented, and resourceful. For instance, he was an academic, played musical instruments (piano and guitar), and was a vocalist and a computer nerd. My life changed after his tutelage and mentorship. One prime thing he taught me, which I will not forget, is the power of writing down goals. There's psychology in writing things down.

If you want to cook, you study cooking and you follow the rules and principles regarding the combining of ingredients and its preparations. So it applies if you want to achieve success in your area of endeavor. Follow the rules and principles of successful people, as success leaves clues. Their more common quality is that they're intensely action-oriented. They're proactive rather than reactive – they take initiative.

There is a story of a man who decides to commit a suicide by jumping off a thirty-storey building. As he plunges toward the ground, someone leans out of a fifteenth-storey window and shouts, "How's it going?" The falling man shouts back, "So far, so good!"

I have achieved the goal of writing this book (after many hits and misses, many errors, and much failure), and I encourage you to take the leap of faith toward those nice goals you have in mind. This book is a collection of everything I learned and my experience of moving from nothing to something. The simple truth is that: **You Can Do It Too!**

These principles and techniques have not only worked for me, but they have also worked for other people who have reached out with their testimonies of their new selves. I guarantee you will be positively transformed after journeying with me in this book.

The principles work if you work on them; thus, they won't work if you don't work on them. The fundamentals are the same for all people and all professions. Develop your ability to examine, to evaluate and to discern; these are skills that are more valuable than ever. However, everyone learns differently, and you know how you learn best. *Think and Thank* can be read in these ways:

- As you are reading, underline and highlight everything that feels important to you and make notes in the margin;

- Review those notes and highlighted sections again and again;

- Repetition is the key to real learning; do not read this book just once – if you really want to get the best out of it, go through it again, at least twice, paying rapt attention;

- As you read and reread, remind yourself what you intend to "command" out of life – your goals.

Note: Don't stop reading if you are not familiar with a particular concept or word. Instead, keep an index card or circle that section for later. Don't doubt the principles. It is in human nature to always fear and criticize what we don't understand or what we are not familiar with, but don't fall into that temptation. Remember that you need a **breakdown for a breakthrough.** If there is no action, there will be no result, no venture, no success. As you read to discover the principles to actualize your dream, your potential, and your goals, you will **think** and **thank**!

Use what you learn here. Let's journey together.

PART ONE
JUST THINK

CHAPTER ONE

Stop Worrying, Start Thinking

"Failure does not mean you're a failure;
it just means you haven't succeeded yet."

—Robert H. Schuller

Worry: What Is It?

In 2002, when I was doing an internship program, I met a lady who worried over so many things – not having money for further education, not having a job (be it white or blue collar), not having enough money to cater to her daily needs, eating the same foods every day, and others too numerous to mention. For her, the "it can't be done" became a Rock of Gibraltar. She was among those who could not strike out the "not" in CANNOT. For her, all hope for the future was lost. If I gave her a name, it would be "worry-aholic." Happily, the whole story changed after a tête-à-tête.

Many of us struggle on a daily basis with worry about loss of love, getting old, criticism, poverty, ill health, and even death. Napoleon Hill considered these the six most dangerous enemies we will encounter in life. I am compelled to call this "the inescapability of worry."

It is written in the Biblical text to cease from worry and be not afraid; the Bible verses help you combat fear and uncertainty with messages of hope, reassurance, and guidance. So why worry over what you may not change? In the Bible, Matthew writes:

> Without warning a storm broke over the lake, so violent
> that the waves were breaking right over the boat. But he

was asleep. So, they went to him and woke him saying, save us, Lord, we're going down! And he said to them, why are you so frightened, you men of little faith? And with that, he stood up and rebuked the winds and the sea… Matt. 8:23-26.

In the scripture above, the emphasis lies on the word "frightened," which also translates to feeling fear or worry. And the question is, why are you so frightened? Echoing the voice of Jesus, I ask you why . . . what are you worried about?

When we knock worry out of our minds, we will experience inner peace.

It's Not Academic; Make it Your Treasure Instead

"I beg your pardon! What's this all about?" So shout the voices of the academics, who in their curiosity wish to know the relevance of this book to their academic career. *Think and Thank* isn't for classwork, nor is it meant for academic purposes. Instead, it is a book to be treasured, as it originates from experiences and conversations with the Grand Masters.

When I was younger and was still attending school with my siblings, there was a mantra that my father used to recite: "My child, soak your rosary in water." This means, "Don't worry." I have come to realize as an adult that Daddy was simply echoing the religious words "Courage, don't worry."

Ask yourself this question: Is what I worry about sure to happen? What I fear the most, will it come to me?

We worry ourselves to death. A loving husband who accompanies his wife to the hospital to deliver her baby is worried about her while she's still in the delivery room. A caring mother is worried about her son who climbs up a tree. A student is worried about their upcoming examinations. We are plagued by worries and fears and "what ifs," and they are a normal part of human life.

Sharing from a personal experience, I have always been unwilling to settle as an "idiota" or in "mediocrity," and, motivated to leave the university campus, I embarked on an adventure to learn extra-academic skills. Around June of 2012, in the quest to satisfy my linguistic curiosity and my love for languages, I enrolled in a six-week French class at L'Alliance Francaise. Because of the restrictions (like not leaving the school premise without getting approval from school authorities) surrounding the academic institution I attended at the time, I was concerned about the possibility of combining my major course in the university and the French classes. However, I overcame the fear by registering under a private tutor, at a cost too exorbitant for a student, but I paid and started the French class. At the end of the day, I was happy because the fear of enrolling in the French class while studying my major was conquered. Mahatma Gandhi opines that with the **belief** that you can do it comes the **capacity** to do it, even if it may not seem hopeful at the beginning.

I had the belief and capacity, but the main challenge was taking the French examination. I had the opportunity to learn French when I was in secondary school, but I wanted to learn and speak the language to the native speakers' standard, which required learning in the appropriate environment. The exam was scheduled when school was in session, which brought another worry. As if that was not enough, I had a course examination I had to prepare for, which left me in a difficult situation. But I kept reminding myself that "where there is a will, there is a way."

When the school timetable was published, the date for the French examination did not clash with the second semester examination timetable for my major course, thereby giving me the chance to participate in both exams. I had to request permission from the school authority (because it was a boarding school) to allow me to go for the French exam. It wasn't easy for me, but I kept going. This made me develop my own maxim that "whatever doesn't kill a man, toughens him."

I was successful in the exam. It was a thing of joy when I received a phone call from my French tutor congratulating me, saying, "*C'est tres formidable!*" Imagine how happy I was: my second worry was relieved.

Don't worry – **think** that it is going to work and most of the time it does work.

Your Six Most Dangerous Enemies

"Nothing can bring you peace but yourself," says Dr. Napoleon Hill. What you perceive yourself to be is what you become. Every person on earth is afraid of or worried about something. Although most of our fears are inherited, others are a result of human habits. Our fears (whether inherited or habitual) must be mastered before we can win in any worthwhile undertaking in life because an enemy discovered is an enemy half-whipped.

But why only six enemies? Why not seven, eight, nine, et cetera? This is because they are the basic fears of humankind from which all other small or lesser fears emanate. Hill described them as the most dangerous or basic fears of humankind. In reading through these ugly fears, analyze yourself and find out which of them does you the most damage. My sole intention is to help you throw off these unseen fears, as I have done myself, just like the biblical Saint Paul would talk about putting off the old man.

The Six Most Dangerous Enemies of Humankind

1. Worry about Poverty
2. Worry about Old Age
3. Worry about Ill Health
4. Worry about Criticism
5. Worry about Loss of Love
6. Worry about Death

There are other worries that we encounter in life but through experience and research, I've observed that these are the basis from which other ones originate. As we explain the "enemies" below, take inventory of your own fears and worries and classify them under these six headings.

Worry about Poverty

In writing this section, I spoke with a cousin about one of her major worries in life. "MONEY," she bluntly said. In other words, finances. She fears being poor; it worries her. Most of us might be sharing the same feelings.

It requires courage to tell the truth about the origin of this worry, and still greater courage to accept the truth after it has been told. In calling a spade a spade, Hill pinpoints that the worry of poverty grew out of man's inherited tendency to prey upon his fellow man economically. Nearly all forms of lower animals have instinct but appear not to have the power to reason and think; thus, they prey upon one another physically.

Humans, with their superior sense of intuition, thought, and reason, do not eat their fellow man bodily; rather they get more satisfaction out of eating them financially. So great an offender are humans in this respect that nearly every state and nation has been obliged to pass laws, scores of laws, to protect the weak from the strong. It is on record that of all the ages of the world (the ages about which we know) the current age in which we live seems to be one of money worship. It is a time that humans are considered less than the dust of the earth unless they can display a fat bank account.

Many believe that nothing brings human beings as much suffering and humiliation as poverty; this is why we worry about poverty. After all, who wants to settle as an "economic idiota" who people call nobody. Many marriages have their beginning and often their ending solely on the basis of the wealth possessed by one or both of the contracting parties. This explains why the divorce courts are busy! For some, the word "society" could quite properly be spelled as "$ociety" because it is inseparably associated with the dollar mark. So eager is a person to possess wealth that they will acquire it in whatever manner, whether it's legal or otherwise.

The worry about poverty is a terrible thing. For instance, a man may commit murder, engage in robbery, rape, and all other manners of violation of the rights of others and still regain a high station in the minds of his fellow men, provided he doesn't lose a dime of his wealth. Poverty, therefore, is a crime, an unforgivable sin, as it were. Scripturally, it was as a result of the worry/fear of poverty and possibly hunger that Jacob sent his sons to Egypt to buy grains.

One part of the story goes thus:

> "Jacob, seeing that there was grain for sale in Egypt, said to his sons, why do you stand looking at one another? I hear that there's grain for sale in Egypt; go down and buy grain for us there, that we may survive and not die" (Gen. 42:1-2).

Every state book (like *The Laws of Success* by Napoleon Hill) in the world bears evidence that the worry about poverty is one of the six basic fears of humankind, for in every such book are various laws intended to protect the weak from the strong. To spend time trying to prove either that the worry about poverty is one of man's inherited worries or that this worry has its origin in man's nature to cheat his fellow man would be similar to trying to prove that three times two is six.

When you maintain a grasp on the idea that you are incapable, then failure and loss becomes inevitable. Develop the ability to believe while also telling yourself that you are born to be a winner.

Worry about Old Age

It was Saint Paul who explicitly said, "When you're young, you will dress and go wherever you intend to go, but when you are old, a cord will be tied around your waist while you will be taken to where you don't intend going." (Jn. 21:18-19)

A story was once old of an elderly man – a father – telling his son to take life easy. So, the boy said, "Dad, you're now old school." This means that because of the father's age, he didn't see him as making and talking sense.

The worry about old age, as some scholars say, grows out of two major causes. A story told by Rev. Fr. Dr. Eugene Azorji (who was my professor in Nigeria) comes to mind. There was a religious leader in Nigeria who was very respected because of his intellectual sagacity and verbal-linguistic intelligence or genius but he could not recognize anybody nor recall anything from memory in his old age.

It is no surprise that Drs. Allen D. Bragdon and David Gamon, in *Use it or Lose it: How to Keep Your Brain Fit as it Ages,* talk of the problems facing the aging society. One of the most prominent healthcare concerns these days, they note, is Alzheimer's disease (AD). In their estimation, just thirty years ago, it was considered a rarity; now, four million people have it in the US alone. They predict that over the next twenty years, the number of people with the disease will go up by a factor of three.

The fact remains that each of us find it unbearable that simply by aging we could lose our personality, our enjoyment of life, our memory, and ultimately our social acceptability. All old people tend to experience memory loss or forgetfulness and occasional difficulty learning new tasks (for example, how to use a computer). As a way of reinvigoration, this worry grows out of two sources.

First, that old age may bring with it poverty. Second, and by far the most common source, from false and cruel sectarian teachings that have been so well mixed with "fire and brimstone" that human beings fear old age because it means the approach of another and possibly a much more horrible world than this one, which is already bad enough (Christianity calls this "hell"). A person might fear the unknown aspects of death or just "disappearing."

In the worry about old age, human beings have two very justifiable reasons:

1. Distrust of fellow humans who may seize whatever worldly wealth they possess

2. Terrible pictures of the world to come, which were deeply planted in their minds through socialization and heredity, long before they came into possession of that mind.

Given this, is it any wonder that people fear the approach of old age? In the Igbo (a major ethnic group in Nigeria) traditional belief, any old man nearing the age of sixty to eighty-five who has no male child is greatly worried and troubled because he knows that immediately after he is confirmed dead, his belongings and properties will be shared among the relatives. This is partly because in Igbo culture, lineage is typically patrilineal, meaning that family names and inheritance pass through the male line. Having a male child ensures the continuation of the family name and lineage. The Nigerian (and African-celebrated) literary scholar Chinua Achebe, in *Things Fall Apart*, explains this Igbo ideology in more detail.

Another example is what happened in the scripture between Tobit (the father) and Tobias (the son); Tobit remembered the silver that he had left with Gabael at Rhages in Media and thought, "I've come to the point of praying for death; I should do well to call my son Tobias and tell him about the money before I die." He summoned his son Tobias and told him, "Now, my child, I must tell you I've left ten talents of silver with Gabael son of Garias, at Rhages in Media. Don't be afraid, my child, if we've grown poor" (Tb. 4:1-3; 20-23).

Worry about Ill Health

In 1998, I broke my left hand climbing a coconut tree to bring down dead leaves that were to serve as firewood. Imagine the worry that my mom and dad went through. Another incident occurred around 1996, when my younger brother got a knock on his head from a coconut fruit. There and then, he fainted. Kudos to my grandma, who grabbed him, poured chilly water on him, rubbed Aboniki balm (a special and traditional kind of substance for quick relief of aches and pain) on his body, and laid him on a mat inside the house for him to regain his strength. Fortunately, after some hours of sleeping and resting, he woke up.

My mom (Dad was away for work) was so worried she thought my brother wouldn't survive. That incident made me realize that worry could make people not think of or feel hunger. This may apply to the worry about ill health.

For Hill, this worry is born out of both physical and social heredity. Right from birth until death, there is external warfare within every physical body; that is, warfare between groups of cells, one group being known as the friendly builders of the body, and the other as the destroyers, or "disease germs." The seed of fear is born in the physical body as the result of nature's plan of permitting the stronger forms of cell life to prey upon the weaker. Social heredity has played its part through the lack of cleanliness and knowledge of sanitation, and also through the law of suggestion cleverly manipulated by those who profited from ill health.

The worry about ill health has its origin, to a considerable extent, in the same sources as the fears of poverty and old age. This is simply because it also leads toward the unknown pathway of which humans have heard some discomforting stories. Because of this, people even worry themselves to "death" when they hear that someone is in a coma – a deep, unconscious state, usually lasting a long time and caused by serious illness or injury. By worrying about ill health, a person might be concerned about how society might receive and respond to them.

Worry about Criticism

Sam Deep and Lyle Sussman, in *Yes, You Can!*, reporting on Norman Vincent Peale, believe that "most of us would rather be ruined by praise than be saved by criticism." It is only martyrs (those who suffer very much or are killed because of their religious or political beliefs) and masochists (people who enjoy something that most people would find unpleasant or painful) that enjoy censure. The rest of us respond like children eating spinach; we know it's good for us, but we don't like it.

However, unless we understand that it is only a tree with ripe fruits that receives the greatest number of stone throws, we will not untie ourselves from the shackles of the worry of criticism. One of my good friends during my studies in Nigeria told me how his mom was worried about his attempt to upskill himself. He was caught in the middle between whether to please his mom or acquire the skill. He was worried and feared criticism, not only from his mom but also from school friends. Just how a human being acquired this basic worry would be hard, if not impossible, to determine, but one thing is certain – he had it well developed.

Digging deeper into this fear, some believe that this worry made its appearance in the mind of humans about the time that politics came into existence. Others believe its source could be traced no further than the first meeting of an organization of females known as a "Women's Club," that is, an organized group/setting where social dynamics and opinions are strongly felt and expressed, thereby contributing to the development of the fear of being criticized. Still another school of humorists links the origin to the content of the Holy Bible, whose pages abound with some very vitriolic and violent forms of criticism. In analyzing this, if the latter claim is correct, and those who believe literally all they find in the Bible aren't mistaken, the question a critical mind might ask is: could God be responsible for man's inherent fear of criticism since God inspired the writing of the scripture?

Dr. Hill attributes fear to that part of man's inherited nature that prompts him not only to take away his fellow man's goods and wares but also to justify his action by criticism of his fellow man's character. Fear takes on many different forms, the majority of which are petty and trivial. Let's share the experience of Mr. Solomon, a friend during my studies in Nigeria. Solomon was not just a friend, but also a mentor.

During our studies, he shared with me some critiques he received from his classmates and friends. Because of his unique approach to things, he was given different sorts of names, one of which was "a pagan"; pagan has a derogative meaning within the Nigerian environment. He didn't mind these things, which he tagged "sidetracks," because he was focused on his goals. FOCUS here means **Follow One Course Until Successful**. The irony happened when after acquiring those skills, these "sycophants" were the first to request his services. I was not left behind in this train of criticism, being a student of Solomon, a goal-setter and an achiever. My criticisms came from classmates, friends, and even family. Whatever people don't understand, they criticize.

Using a Biblical reflection, Joseph (the dreamer) was not left behind. Here's a little excerpt of his story:

> Jacob loved Joseph more than all his other sons, for he was the son of his old age, and he had a coat with long sleeves made for him. Now Joseph had a dream, and he repeated it to his brothers. Listen, he said to this dream I have had; we were binding sheaves in the countryside, and my sheaf, it seemed, rose up and stood upright, and I saw your sheaves gather round and bow to my sheaf. So, you want to be king over us – said his brothers; and they hated him still more, on account of his dreams and of what he said (Gen. 37:3-11).

Joseph's brothers didn't criticize him, but they hated him. Yes, criticism breeds hatred and other vices; once people criticize you it means that you're two steps ahead of them.

Worry about the Loss of Love

"My heart is broken," echoes the voices of today's men and women. The source from which this worry originated needs little description, for it is obvious it grew out of man's nature to steal his fellow man's mate, or at least to take liberties with her, unknown to her rightful "lord" and master, as I have observed and learned.

So many people can go to extremes because of the loss of the love of a girlfriend, fiancée, fiancé, husband, or wife. Worry about the loss of Juliet, Romeo's lover in Shakespeare's *Romeo and Juliet*, made the play a memorable work of literature. Romeo was ready to do anything humanly possible to keep Juliet.

There is little doubt that jealousy and all other similar forms of insanity grew out of people's inherited worry about the loss of someone's love. The simplest way to explain and understand this fear (based on research) is an ancient and strange story of a man who was jealous of a woman, and a woman who was jealous of a man. This fills the divorce courts and causes murder and other forms of cruel punishment. It is a holdover, handed down through social heredity, from the Stone Age, when man preyed upon his fellow man, stealing his mate by physical force. The method, not the practice, has now changed to some extent. Nowadays, instead of physical force man steals his fellow man's mate with pretty, colorful cars and stately mansions.

Human beings are improving; man now "entices" where once he "drove." The scripture says:

> When famine came to the land Abram (who was later renamed Abraham) went down into Egypt to stay there for a time, since the land was hard pressed by the famine. On the threshold of Egypt, he said to his wife Sarai (later renamed Sarah): "Listen, I know you're a beautiful woman. When the Egyptians see you, they will say, that's his wife, and they will kill me but spare you. Tell them you're my

sister, so that they may treat me well because of you and spare my life out of regard for you. (Gen. 12:10-13).

Without mincing words, it's simply because of the loss of the love of Sarah that Abraham came up with the idea. Such is the worry about the loss of the love of someone.

Worry about Death

Are you ready to die? Do you want to say goodbye to your loved ones right now? I would assume the answer to the question is no! I can imagine you responding to the question by saying "you're crazy," "you don't understand what you're saying," "I reject that," "over my dead body," etc. At the sound of death, our bodies cringe. The death that I will explain here is what could be called "untimely death." But is there any death that is untimely?

For tens of thousands of years, human beings have been asking the still-unanswered questions "whence" and "whither?" The craftiest of the race have not been slow to offer the answer to the eternal question: "Where did I come from and where am I going after death?" Hill writes, "Come into my tent and you may go to heaven after death." Here, Heaven was pictured as a wonderful city whose streets were lined with gold and studded with precious stones. The second part goes thus: "Remain out of my tent and you may go straight to hell." Hell was pictured as a blazing furnace where the poor victim might have the misery of burning forever in brimstone. Hence comes our fear of and worry about death.

To many, this is the worst of all the "six enemies." Echoing the voice of scholars, in truth, no person knows, and nobody has ever known, what heaven or hell is like, and this very lack of definite knowledge opens the door of the human mind, with its stock of legerdemain and various brands of trickery, deceit, and fraud. Biblically, there is heaven and hell. Most of what we know (if not all) about heaven and hell has been based on the biblical injunction that says:

If these people die a natural death such as men commonly die, then Yahweh hasn't sent me. But if Yahweh does something utterly, if the earth should open its mouth and

> swallow them, themselves and all that belongs to them, so that they go down alive to Sheol, then you will know that these men have been rejected; the ground split open under their feet, the earth opened its mouth and swallowed them, their families too, and all Korah's men and all their belongings. They went down alive to Sheol, they and all their possessions. The earth closed over them, and they disappeared from the midst of the assembly (Num. 16:29-33).

The New Testament (NT) says:

> When the Son of Man comes in his glory, escorted by all the angels, then he will take his seat on his throne of glory. All the nations will be assembled before him, and he will separate men one from another as the shepherd separates sheep from goats. Then the king will say to those on his right hand, come, you whom my Father has blessed, take for your heritage the kingdom prepared for you since the foundation of the world. Next, he will say to those on his left hand, go away from me, with you curse upon you, to the eternal fire prepared for the devil and his angels (Matt. 25:31-42).

The truth is that no person knows nor has anybody ever known where we come from at birth or where we go to at death. Anyone claiming the "whence" and "whither" of death is either deceiving themselves or he is a conscious impostor who makes it a business to live without rendering service of value through playing upon the credulity of humanity.

From the study of the ideas of Napoleon Hill, the first step to take in "killing off" these enemies is to find out **Where** and **How** you acquired them. They could have gotten their grip on you through two forms of heredity:

1. Physical heredity (to which Charles Darwin devoted much study)
2. Social heredity, through which the fears, superstitions, and beliefs of people who lived during the Dark Ages have been passed on from one generation to another.

In the beginning, we find that nature has been a cruel builder from the lowest form of life to the peak (its highest point); nature has permitted the stronger to prey upon the weaker forms of animal life. The Old Testament verse (Gen. 25:23) says: "There are two nations in your womb, your issues will be two rival peoples. One nation shall have the mastery of the other and the elder shall serve the younger." This lays credence to the aforementioned statement. The fish prey upon the worms and insects, eating them. Birds prey upon the fish. Higher forms of animal life prey upon the birds, all the way up the line to human beings. Thus, the weaker forms of animal life have learned to fear and worry about the stronger ones. This fear or worry consciousness is inherent in every living animal; the hen is pretty worried at the sight of either the kite or hawk. However, in the higher animal (humans), the poor and wretched are worried and conscious of the rich. Humans prey upon all the other lower forms of animal life, even upon their fellows.

The whole story of evolution is one unbroken chain of evidence of cruelty and destruction of the weaker by the stronger. This, I would think, applies to the spiritual realm – the supra-human level having reflected on the scriptural passage that says:

> "When he reached the country of the Gadarenes on the other side, two demoniacs came towards him out of the tombs – creatures so fierce that no one could pass that way. They stood there shouting, what do you want with us, Son of God? Have you come here to torture us before the time?" (Matt. 8:28-30).

Examining social heredity and what part it has played in our human make-up, the term, says Hill, refers to everything that is taught, everything we learn or gather from observation and experience with other living beings.

Know the Reason Why

The Igbo people of Nigeria have a maxim that says, "A person who doesn't know where the rain starts beating them will not know where it will stop beating them." To elaborate on this, during my undergraduate studies in Nigeria (as a member of a religious group called Legion of Mary), a friend was asked to give a speech during one of our regular meetings about the "reason why" we do what we do. In our effort to know the "reason why" for all our worries, we have to give up all our excuses. George Washington Carver, a chemist who discovered over 325 uses for the peanut, believes that "99% of all failures come from people who have a habit of making excuses." The majority of us don't take 100% responsibility of our life; thus, we indulge in worries, most of which are trivial. Sometimes we blame the outside circumstances as being behind our worries. We have the power to control what goes into and out of our minds, which is the motivating force behind human action. To take mastery of the mind is to take mastery over our worries. You have to take the position that you have always had the power to make it different, to get it right, and to produce the desired result.

The tip of the iceberg is that most people are still slaves of the past; they are still living in what Dale Carnegie calls "STD," which means Stupid Things Done. One day, two monks were traveling for a mission. Before they left their community they were instructed and prohibited by their master from touching or even looking at any girl. In the course of their journey through a deserted place, they came across a pond; as they were passing by the side of the pond, they saw a girl who was already in the pond and was about to drown. On seeing her in that helpless situation, one of the monks, remembering the instructions of their master, instantly closed his eyes and turned his face away since they were prohibited from looking at or touching a girl. But the second monk couldn't turn his eyes away from the girl who was almost drowning. Being moved by pity, he jumped into the pond, caught hold of the drowning girl, and brought her out to safety. Getting out of the pond, the monk discovered that the girl had become unconscious, and out of pity he decided to give her an artificial respiration in order to save her life. After some effort, the girl was resuscitated, and when he saw that she was all right, he went to meet his colleague and they continued their journey back to their master's place.

After about one week of their journey, when they were about to reach their master's place, the monk that had closed his eyes at the sight of the drowning girl broke the silence and said to the other monk, "Hey, you have broken the discipline and disobeyed the master's instruction. Not only did you look at the girl, but you also touched her and carried her in your arms."

The other monk listened carefully and patiently, smiled at him, then said, "Yes, my dear friend, you are actually right. I even touched her and carried her in my arms. But I did all this only for a couple of minutes or so. As soon as I dropped the girl from my arms, I took everything that happened away from my heart. I've even forgotten about it, whereas you're still carrying her in your mind." Many of us are like the first monk; we have the habit of carrying our past memories for many years even when the incident may have lost its relevance. If something doesn't turn out as planned, would you keep worrying and then kill yourself? My findings recommend the following exercise:

- How did I create that?
- What was I thinking?
- What were my beliefs?
- What did I say or not say?
- What did I do or not do to create that result?
- How did I get the other person to act that way?
- What do I need to do differently next time to get the result I want?

Jack Canfield, a notable American author and speaker, presents a formula:

Event + Response = Outcome.

This illustrates that life's outcomes, whether they are positive or negative, stem from our reactions to past events. To change undesirable results, one can either blame the circumstances (E) or alter their responses (R) to these events to achieve the desired outcome (O).

If you are an alcoholic wanting to stop drinking in order to make your life better but keep on drinking, your life isn't going to get any better! Take charge and take control. The day you change your responses is the day your life will begin to get better.

Robert H. Schuller talked about **IPDE**, which stands for: **I**dentify, **P**redict, **D**ecide, and **E**xecute

The IPDE prescription can help you in knowing the "reason why" you face a variety of problems, by putting a "stop-loss" to your worries. Identify the problem; predict what this problem will do to you if you don't do anything about it; decide on your response from all the options and alternatives, then execute and act on the most positive option you can imagine.

The Magic Wand: Ask, Ask, Ask

The Magic Wand (that is transformative principle) of asking may not be a new thing to most people. To some, it may sound like:

- A way of making inquiries
- A way of persuasion/request
- Both

This real conversation between me and my friend, Gloria, centers on having a great deal of ideas but without financial support to execute them. This will help convey the meaning and application of the first part of the Magic Wand.

Gloria: Life hasn't been easy for me, especially after high school. Please, I need your assistance.

JB: It's the same everywhere – it has not been easy for anybody. Nothing is difficult except the things that we make so. Please, my dear, how may I help you?

Gloria: Ouch! No, no, no. I strongly believe that there's a way, just like Don Moen sang: "God will make a way where there seems to be no way" but that way is what is obscured to me. Also, being an experienced person, I do believe you have some answers for me.

JB: (After a little pause) Okay. What are your plans and your goals?

Gloria: (Without wasting time) I want to go to university and become a musician and writer.

JB: I am asking you about your goal partly to share with you some of my findings on the importance of setting goals. In researching Robert Kiyosaki's books – for example, *Rich Dad Poor Dad*, I found he says, "an entrepreneur should have a mission." So, also, a successful person should have a goal, be purposeful and mission-oriented. I would recommend you use **OPM.** Have you heard of it before?

Gloria: (After a little pause) I beg your pardon, OPM? What does it mean?

JB: Well, that is the secret behind the success of most business moguls, even multibillionaires. This simply means *Other Peoples' Money*. Some people, like Robert G. Allen, call it *OPR – Other Peoples' Resources*. Meanwhile, what can you tell me about your family?

Gloria: I have siblings; they aren't strong financially. As for my relatives, I have nothing much to say (she smiles).

JB: Could you help me to understand what you mean by you have "nothing much to say"?

Gloria: I'm just afraid of my relatives; I feel like it won't work to ask them for help.

JB: You just have the feeling it won't work, right?

Gloria: Yes, but –

JB: But have you tried it? See, most of our failures come as we condemn ourselves before others condemn us. You are not a failure unless you think so. Most people are out to lend a helping hand to us as far as we are able to stretch out our receiving hand. The Bible says:

> . . .then Peter got out of the boat and started walking towards Jesus across the water, but as soon as he felt the force of the wind, he took fright and began to sink. Lord, save me! He cried. Jesus put out his hand at once and held him. (Matt.14:27-33)

Dr. Napoleon Hill explains the first magic wand with a story called "Three Feet from Gold." For Hill, one of the most common causes of failure is the habit of quitting when one is overtaken by temporary defeat. An abridged version of the story as told by Dr. Hills is as follows:

R.U. Darby, who later became one of the most successful insurance salesmen in the United States of America, tells the story of his uncle, who was caught by the "gold fever" in the gold-rush days and went west to dig and grow rich. He had never heard the saying that "more gold has been mined from the brains of men than has ever been taken from the earth." He staked a claim and went to work with a pick and shovel. The going was hard, but his lust for gold was definite.

After weeks of labor, he was rewarded with the discovery of the shining ore. He needed machinery to bring the ore to the surface. Quietly, he covered up the mine, returned his footsteps to his home in Williamsburg, Maryland, and told his relatives and a few neighbors of the "strike." They got together money for the needed machinery and had it shipped. The uncle and Darby went back to work at the mine.

The first car of ore was mined and shipped to a meter. The returns proved they had one of the richest mines in Colorado! A few more cars of that ore would clear the debts. Then would come the big killing in profits. Down went the drills! Up went the hopes of Darby and uncle! Then something happened – the vein of gold ore disappeared. They had come to the end of the rainbow, and the pot of gold was no longer there. They drilled on, desperately trying to pick up the vein again, all to no avail.

Finally, they decided to quit. They sold the machinery to a junk man for a few hundred dollars and took the train back home. Some junk men are dumb, but not this one! He called in a mining engineer to look at the mine and do a little calculating. The engineer advised that the project had failed because the owners weren't familiar with fault lines. His calculations showed that the vein would be found just three feet from where the Darbys had stopped drilling! That's exactly where it was found. In simple words, the Darbys failed because they ignored making inquiries while the "junk man" succeeded because he made inquiries. In other words, you're not a failure – you haven't failed yet; you're just three feet from gold.

This age-old secret of saying goodbye to worries – the secret to becoming successful – has been in use right before and during the time of Jesus Christ. Also, many people – myself included – are always in the habit of using **OPM** (or OPR) and **OPT** (Other Peoples' Time), which is a way of asking. And Jesus says:

> So, I say to you, ask and it will be given to you; search and you will find; knock and the door will be opened for you. For the one who asks always receives; the one who searches always finds; the one who knocks will always have the door opened to him (Lk. 11:9-10).

The New Testament text is filled with people who use this Magic Wand to quench their thirst. For instance, Peter asked to walk on water (Matt. 14:28-29); the Canaanite woman asked for her daughter to be healed (Matt.15:21-28); the mother of Zebedee's sons made her request (Matt. 20:20-21); the lost "prodigal" son asked his father to accept him back (Lk. 11-24), and many others.

You've got to ask. Asking is the world's most powerful and neglected secret to success and happiness, says Percy Ross (a self-made multimillionaire and philanthropist). History is filled with examples of incredible riches and astounding benefits people have received simply by asking for them. If you're like most people, you may be holding yourself back by not asking for the information, assistance, support, money, and time that you need to fulfill your vision and make your dreams come true, thereby overcoming your worries.

But wait a minute – if it sounds this simple, why are people afraid to ask? I believe people are afraid of many things, such as:

- Looking needy
- Looking foolish
- Looking stupid
- Experiencing rejection
- Hearing the word NO

One day I heard my mom saying that the reason she didn't ask people for things was because of hearing the ugly word "NO." The sad thing is that people actually reject themselves in advance; that is, people are saying "NO" to themselves before anyone else even has a chance to.

But how can a person ask to get what they need and say farewell to worries? While researching *How to Get from Where You Are to Where You Want to Be* by Jack Canfield, I learned that there's a specific science to asking for and getting what you want or need in life. Some of the quick tips include:

- Ask as if you expect to get it; that is, ask with a positive expectation of "yes."
- Assume you can; that is, act as if you have already gotten it.
- Ask someone who can give it to you; that is, seek expert or professional advice.
- Be clear and specific, as portrayed in the conversation between me and Gloria.
- Ask repeatedly, just like the biblical unscrupulous judge and the importunate woman

(who kept asking many times in an annoying way) (Lk.18:1-8).

Nothing happens until you act. "If your ship doesn't come in, swim out to meet it," says Jonathan Winters (Grammy Award-winning comedian, actor, writer, and artist). To demonstrate the power of this Magic Wand, Jack Canfield explains that in his seminar, he held up a $100 bill and asked, "Who wants this $100 bill?" Most of the people in the audience raised their hands, and some waved their hands vigorously back and forth while others shouted out, "I just want it" or "I'll take it" or "Give it to me." He stood there calmly holding out the bill until eventually, someone jumped out of her seat, rushed to the front of the room, and took the bill from his hand.

After the person sat down, now $100 richer for her efforts, he asked the audience, "What did this person do that no one else in the room did?" She got up and acted. She did what was necessary to get the money, and that is exactly what you must do if you want to say goodbye to your worries. Experience the power of the Magic Wand – you have nothing to lose but everything to gain by asking, asking, asking.

Maybe it's Just Emotion

In one of Cedric M. Kenny's books, *Study Smart Score High,* he tries to show the difference between primates from Homo sapiens (the species or kind of human being that exists now). Someone said in every classroom there are dullards, average kids, and brilliant ones. The question is, are kids born average, dull, or brilliant? If you take a look at newborn infants lying in rows of cots in the hospital nursery, would you point a finger at one infant and say, "Look, he's a dull one, or see, over there, that one looks brilliant"?

As Kenny explains further, we don't go about hammering labels on cots. All the infants look "normal" because they're normal babies. Yet sadly, a few years later, when they go to school, many of these normal kids will crack down under academic pressure; they will be labeled as average, intelligent, or dullards. Then the simple but difficult question is, why does that happen?

Temperament – the combination of traits we inherited from our parents – influences everything you do, from eating habits, driving skills, the way you shop, yard care, study habits, to other daily habits/activities. For instance, Tim LaHaye says, "I can almost judge a man's temperament by his eating habits." In trying to bring to the limelight the influence of temperament on everything we do, he tells a story:

When he was in high school, there was a pair of identical twins in his class. Students could hardly tell them apart. They assessed out identically on their IQ scores (128). But that was where their similarities stopped. One was personable, the other withdrew from people. One loved sports, history, and literature; the other preferred math, physics, and language. Interestingly, their grade point averages were almost identical at the end of their four years in high school. Yet they didn't get the same grades in most subjects. What made the difference between these young men? Their temperaments. According to LaHaye, as a human, there's no other influence in your life more powerful than your temperament.

Know your temperament(s) and direct or take control of its style of worrying. What are temperaments and the temperamental disposition to fear, in other words, worry? Nothing has a more profound influence on your behavior than your inherited temperament. According to research (for instance, R. Plomin, J.C. DeFries, and J.C. Loehlin in "Genotype-environmental interaction and correlation in the analysis of human behavior"), the combination of your parents' genes and chromosomes at conception, which determine your basic temperament nine months before you drew your first breath, is largely responsible for your actions, reactions, and emotional responses to one degree or another, therefore almost affecting everything you do. It is because of being unaware of this powerful influence that some people say things like, "I don't like myself," or "I can't understand myself."

The fact remains that when a person discovers their own basic temperament, they can manage their own worrying habits. Having a background knowledge of your temperament(s) helps put your style of worry in control. The heart of the temperament theory, as first conceived by Hippocrates over 2400 years ago, divides people into four basic categories, which he named:

- Sanguine temperament
- Choleric temperament
- Melancholy temperament
- Phlegmatic temperament

The **sanguine** talks about the weather, friends, and a hundred things before facing the real problem. The **choleric** gets right to the point. He wants you to help his partner/wife changer their behavior so they can enjoy a better home life. The **melancholy** sighs deeply, with depression, self-pity, and unhappiness etched on his face. The **phlegmatic** rarely gets around to making an appointment, and when he does it takes most of the first half hour just to get him pumped up.

People act the way they do simply because of their temperament or combinations of them. Some of our acts are subtle, like tastes or preferences, while others involve outlooks and attitudes or even styles of thinking. There is hardly a function in life that is not influenced by temperament, including our worrying habits.

Temperament is passed on through the genes and is no doubt influenced by the Adamic fall. That's why we all identify with the desire to do good while at the same time we possess a desire to do evil. The apostle Paul no doubt felt that same way when he said:

> For though the will to do what is good is in me, the performance is not, with the result that instead of doing the good things I want to do, I carry out the sinful things I don't want. When I act against my will, then, it's not my true self doing it, but sin which lives in me (Rom. 7:18-20).

Paul, without mincing a word, differentiated between himself and that uncontrollable form within by saying, "It's not my true self doing it, but sin which lives in me." The "I" is Paul's person (in other words, the soul, will, and mind of man), while the sin that dwelled in him was the human nature that he, like all human beings, inherited from his parents. No wonder this particular trend is given so many names in the Bible: "the natural man," "the flesh," "the old man," and "corruptible flesh." Some psychologists even suggest that we get more genes from our grandparents than from our parents. That could account for the greater resemblance of some children to their grandparents than to their parents.

Once a person diagnoses their own basic temperament, they are in a better position to take care of their style of worry. These four basic temperaments introduce you to the four distinct types of people, but there are blends of temperaments – one usually dominates, while the other remains secondary. For instance, as Dr. Tim LaHaye points out, we have **SanChlor** (that is, SanguineCholeric), **SanMel** (that is, SanguineMelancholy), etcetera. Since this is not a psychology book, we won't dwell on the temperament factor.

Is it true that "what you are emotionally is what you are?" Fr. Azorji says that "when your emotion overrides the sense of reasoning, enmeshment occurs" (that is, the state of mental imbalance). We are emotional creatures; our emotions can influence every area of our lives, positively or negatively. Dr. LaHaye believes that "no matter how intelligent a person is, when he gets emotionally upset, he can't think in an orderly fashion." To support this, Dr. LaHaye tells a story of a professional scholar, who because of anger and depression (emotional culprits) squandered his potential and retired with less prestige and position than he had at twenty-seven.

Human emotions are particularly powerful between the ages of fourteen and twenty-four. That could be the reason the "devil" uses society, education, drugs, friends, and amusements on young people during those years. He knows how vulnerable they are to making bad life decisions when they are most emotional and self-destructive.

As Dr. Hill talks of the "six basic enemies" of man, in like manner, Dr. LaHaye talks of "two emotional culprits." All of us experience many variable emotions in our lifetime, but they stem from two basic roots:

1. Anger
2. Fear or worry

The former isn't our sole priority here; the one that concerns us should be fear and worry. Arguably, fear was the first emotion to surface in the Bible after the fall of Adam. The scripture says, "but Yahweh God called to the man, where are you? He asked. I heard the sound of you in the garden, he replied, "I was afraid" (Gen. 3:9-10).

From my research, I believe that the melancholy and phlegmatic have a fear tendency (while all choleric and sanguine have an anger tendency). Worry is the paralyzing emotion that inhibits or restricts normal feelings of love, confidence, and well-being. It triggers negative thought patterns, breeding anxiety and other emotions that can multiply like a giant snowball and consume a person's entire life. Worry is to your emotions what cancer of the blood is to your body: it invades the whole body. Worry and fear experienced by people when they first do anything dangerous, such as driving a car, motorcycle, or airplane, etc. is different from the worry I emphasize here, which inhibits or restricts people from attempting what they would like to do or should do.

With the knowledge that everyone experiences fear or worry, it is worth mentioning that some people have a greater problem with it than others and that some experience it more than others. According to Dr. LaHaye, the differences to the amount each person experiences fear/worry can be detected in early childhood. The **melancholy** temperament is more intense, lasts longer, occupies more thinking, and inhibits life more, while the **phlegmatics** are simply worriers, which properly limits them. But this doesn't mean that the **choleric** and **sanguine** temperaments do not experience worries; they do, but maybe in smaller proportions.

There is a prevalent and negative pattern of anxiety among humans, and this pattern has its underlying causes or origins from factors like emotional results, social results, and physical results. For your benefit, dear reader, I highlight below eight likely causes of human worries:

- Temperamental disposition
- Childhood experience
- A traumatic experience
- A negative thinking pattern
- Anger
- Sin
- Lack of faith
- Habit

Do you know that you can learn to live without your worries? Since virtue is knowledge, says Socrates, and knowledge can be taught, you can also be taught how to overcome your worries. From a religious perspective, the simple key is to learn to live by faith. I understand that not everyone will accept this advice but some workable, step-by-step procedures to overcome your worries include:

- With good faith, face your worries as sin, for "every act done in bad faith is sin"
- (Rom.14:23.)
- Confess your worry as a sin.
- Ask God to take away the habit of worry.
- Ask for the indwelling of divinity.
- Appreciate God by faith for victory over worry.
- Repeat, repeat, and repeat the above formula.

The simple truth is that these procedures will not work for you until you work on them – give it a try.

Fundamental Facts about Worry

Winston Churchill said, "When I look back on all these worries, I remember the story of the old man who said on his deathbed that he had a lot of trouble in his life, most of which never happened." That's the plain fact of worry. Jack Canfield called it **Fantasized (or False) Experiences Appearing Real – F.E.A.R.**

In *Yes, You Can!* by Sam Deep and Lyle Sussman, they wrote of "Platonic-Socratic" dialogue, the new agora on how to overcome this enemy of humans – worry. They offered some questions for you consider as you worry your life away:

- Is it real?
- What's the evidence that there's really something to worry about?
- Is it something that you can change right now?
- What do you accomplish by worrying about this?
- What can you do to reduce the probability that what you worry about will occur?

Talk over your problems (your worries) with someone who will listen, write about your problems, and jot down some ideas on how to deal with them. Above everything else, I highly recommend you look up Dale Carnegie's *How to Stop Worrying and Start Living*. It is always good to give things a try, especially when it has been researched and proven to work. Try these down-to-earth techniques to chisel away worries, which are the enemies of humans:

- Live in day-tight compartments, that is, simply to focus on the present day and not to worry about the past or the future.
- The magic formula for solving worry situations explained below.
- Worry about basic techniques as explained below.
- Break it before it breaks you.

The Infinite Intelligence (whom I refer to as Jesus Christ) was making sense when He, in the process of teaching Our Lord's Prayer, admonished us to ask: "give us today our daily bread" (Matt. 6:11; Lk. 11:3). Psalm

118:24 says, "This is the day made memorable by Yahweh, what immense joy for us."

Would you like a quick, surefire recipe for handling worrisome situations, a technique you can start using right away? Heed this "magic formula" as pointed out by Willis H. Carrier, which consists of three steps:

1. Analyze the situation fearlessly and honestly and figure out what is the worst that could possibly happen as a result of this worry.

2. After figuring out the worst that could possibly happen, reconcile yourself to accepting it, if necessary.

3. From there, calmly devote your time and energy to trying to improve upon the worst, which you have already accepted mentally. It's important to understand that those who struggle to find solutions to their worries may experience health challenges.

Worry has its basic techniques, which are used to analyze and solve it. Rudyard Kipling opines, "I keep six honest serving men which taught me all I knew. Their names are What and Why, When, How, and Where and Who." Will the thematic formula of Willis H. Carrier solve all worry-related problems? Dr. Dale Carnegie retorts, "no," of course. Thus, I recommend analyzing worry using the following:

Rule 1: Get the facts. Always remember the dictum of Dean Hawkes of Columbia University: "Half of the worry in the world is caused by people trying to make decisions before they have sufficient knowledge on which to base a decision."

Rule 2: After carefully weighing all the facts, come to a decision.

Rule 3: Once a decision is carefully reached, act! Get busy carrying out your decision.

Rule 4: When any of your associates are tempted to indulge in worry about a problem, write out and answer the following questions:

1. What's the problem?

2. What's the cause of the problem?

3. What are all the possible solutions?

4. What's the best solution?

Nature abhors a vacuum. My friend Gloria once said, "When I'm busy, I have no time for worry." Dale Carnegie believes that "it's difficult to worry while you're busy doing something that requires planning and thinking." He tells of a housewife he met from Chicago during the Second World War, who discovered that "the remedy for worry is to get completely occupied doing something constructively."

So, how do you break worry before it breaks you? Follow these rules:

- Don't fuss about trifles. Let's not allow ourselves to be upset by small things we should despise and forget. I have made it my day-to-day maxim when worry crops up to say, "Get concerned about the things that concerns you." Hence this legal maxim says: *De minimus non curat lex* – "the law doesn't concern itself with trifles." Remember that life is too fleeting to dwell on trivialities.

- Ask yourself: what are the odds of these things happening at all?

- Be in rapport with the Infinite Intelligence: God. This implies co-operating with the inevitable. If you know a circumstance is beyond your powers to change it, say to yourself: it's so, it can't be otherwise.

- Put a "stop-loss" order on your worries. Decide how much the worry is worth and refuse to give it anymore.

- Don't saw sawdust. When you start worrying about things that are over and done with, you are merely trying to sow sawdust. Always put this Shakespearean dictum at the back of your mind: "Wise men never sit and wail their loss, but cheerily seek how to redress their harms."

To summarize with Dr. Carnegie's words: "If you were to read everything that has ever been written about worry by the great scholars of all time, you would never read anything more basic or more profound than such hackneyed proverbs as in "don't cross your bridges until you come to them; and don't cry over spilt milk." It was Benjamin Franklin who once said that "knowledge is power." But how useful is that knowledge if not applied? Thus, knowledge isn't power if not applied. Give the above principles and proven facts a chance and see their tremendous and magical powers.

Takeaway from Chapter One

▶ From *ab initio* (in the beginning), the concept of worry has been in existence and has been discussed profoundly by scholars, and especially by Jesus Christ. One of the oldest books, the Bible, has a lot to teach us about worry.

▶ This enemy of humans, worry (or fear) isn't an academic or classroom concept; rather it's a thing that we live with day to day. Know it and put it under control; as James Allen believes, "man is the master."

▶ Experts have streamlined our worries into the "six most dangerous enemies;" get to know yours. If you can't control it, manage it!

▶ Life has its "rule of the game," and so does worry. So, know the reason behind every one of your actions and you say goodbye to your worries.

▶ The Magic Wand has been used by people since the beginning of time; however, it's unfortunate that most people know it but don't use it. How powerful is knowledge if not applied? It's not a metaphysical thing but rather, it's pragmatic. Get rid of worry by starting today: ASK, ASK, ASK.

▶ The secret of every good relationship is understanding; likewise, the simple secret of overcoming your worries is to understand your emotion. Know your temperamental disposition and conquer your worries.

▶ Whatever the mind can conceive and believe, it can achieve, says Dr. Napoleon Hill. Worry has its techniques for getting to you. Get the "master code" and get access to your true, happy life. Enjoy!

CHAPTER TWO

Know Your DCA

"There's one quality which one must possess to win, and that's the definiteness of purpose, the knowledge of what one wants, and a burning desire to possess it."

—Napoleon Hill

The Infinite-Inverse Paradox

Stan Dale (founder of the Human Awareness Institute and author of *Fantasies Can Set You Free*) once said, "I have always been the opposite of a paranoid. I operate as if everyone is part of a plot to enhance my well-being."

Curiosity, they say, is the mother of invention. I once read that it was the curious mind of this Ionian philosopher, Thales, which propelled him to say, "The primary matter of everything is water." After him followed pre-Socratics, who gave divergent views and opinions on the primordial factor behind the existence of things in the universe. Thales was the first to rationalize things, be it human existence and/or the power of the Greek gods. At this point, I encourage you to have an inquisitive mind.

In my curiosity, I perused the works of Felix McDon in *You Can Rise to the Top*, where he explains that there are three groups of human beings on earth:

1. Those who never care about what happens
2. Those who watch things happen
3. Those who make things happen

To which group do you belong?

Those Who Never Care about What Happens

Life, says Archbishop Fulton J. Sheen, is worth living. However, an unexamined life, to Socrates, isn't worth living. In the categories of people, let's classify the first one as the Epicureans – those who believe in eating and drinking now, for tomorrow will take care of itself. This group, in a nutshell, isn't concerned about what happens around them; all their focus is on eating, drinking, sleeping, and rising, leaving all other things in life to take care of themselves.

Involving yourself in any adventure with this group of people amounts to building castles in the air. McDon associates them with this quote "naked I come into this world and naked I shall return."

It still rings like a bell in my mind that some of my classmates used to say during my undergraduate studies that "tomorrow will be better." They exempt themselves from any demanding tasks. For them, why bother when one day you must surely die? This group is what psychologists call **Shallow Minders**. They have no foresight. It is among this group that the *hoi-poloi*, the never-do-wells, are found: they never see beyond their noses. This set of people don't care about paying now to play tomorrow; rather, they live and die in misery, leaving nothing behind that they will be remembered for. In other words, their names are easily forgotten and they easily fizzle away.

This group may be likened to the last servant, whom Jesus Christ condemned in the Bible:

> Sir, said he, I have heard you were a hard man, reaping where you have not sown and gathering where you have not scattered; so, I was afraid, and I went off and hid your talent in the ground. Here it's, it was yours, you have it back. But his master answered him: 'you wicked and lazy servant! (Matt. 25:24-26)

This group are gullible ones who are ready to accept whatever life throws at them.

Those Who Watch Things Happens

There is an old adage that says "he who doesn't know and doesn't know that he doesn't know is a fool; leave him. But he who doesn't know and knows that he doesn't know is asleep; wake him up."

You have probably been to a football game before. What does the arena look like, and what behavior do the fans display? Imagine the kind of uproar and shouting out of different slogans from these mobs, which sometimes might be offensive. The fans either praise a good play or criticize a bad play. It's not in their interest to understand the players' techniques; no, not at all.

The second group are spectators of life. They're fully interested in happenstances and information around them, but never go beyond that. They are only interested in events for watching's sake, but anything more than that emanates from the evil one. They watch and clap their hands for those who are acting on the stage of life for no cost. According to McDon, it is in this set that you have critics whose major preoccupation is to criticize any move that the actors of life make, to judge who is perfect and who is imperfect. In this group, you will probably find gossips who meddle in the affairs of other people. In simple terms, these people only possess the characteristics of judging how good or bad an action is. They don't discuss ideas; rather, they discuss people. Imagine that!

In the real sense, there isn't much difference between this group and the first group, except that the first never cares about what happens around them while the latter are like curious spectators about what happens around them. They live in pain and discontentment every day of their life. They are tepid or lukewarm people.

Those Who Make Things Happen

This group we may refer to as Plato's "philosopher-kings" – the rulers or the aristocrats who dish out laws for a peaceful governing of the state. They are Aristotle's "men of theoria" (that is, men of theory) who the craftsmen and the artisans look up to. By "men," I don't literally mean the male gender – it's gender neutral. These are people like Mandela of South Africa, Gandhi of India, Kwame Nkrumah of Ghana, Marie Curie of Poland, Azikiwe of

Nigeria, and many others. These people are the gladiators of this world. They are the actors of life, the movers and shakers of their societies.

During my undergraduate studies, I often had conversations with a friend called Charles, who identifies himself as a "free thinker." He used to tell me that free thinkers' brains work twenty-four hours a day, seven days a week, 365/366 days a year (around the clock, their brain is in motion). Leaving nothing to chance, they are never satisfied with life throwing anything it wishes at them, and rather they dictate to life what they want, how they want it, when they want it, and where they want it. They have discovered their purpose in life and never settle for less. There are few of my friends who belong to this group of people.

These "men of theoria" believe in the principle that life gives back to you exactly what you put into it. For them, the world is like a bank full of blank checks, where everybody has the right to fill out and collect any amount that pleases them. Some years ago, I had a tête-à-tête with one of my good school friends called James (whom we used to call "DSL"), who once said to me, "My dear, life's too short for you to make your marks." He believes that in every moment, you try to make meaning out of life or the world seems meaningless and absurd.

To live in this world without discovering your purpose for living is to live a life without knowing where you are going; that is, passing through as an ordinary spectator (someone whose major preoccupation is just to sit down and watch the actors/actresses as they play the game of life). You can never discover your purpose when you are noisy and disruptive; you must be able to dig deep into yourself to discover who you are, what you are capable of doing, and what you can't do, your purpose and the discovery of your talents. You are not fit to live only when you have found something worth dying for. True fulfillment comes from discovering something that you are deeply passionate about or believe in, to the extent that you are willing to make the ultimate sacrifice for it.

Some of the questions you can ponder include:

- Among the three groups, where do I belong?
- Which group would I aspire to be in the near future?

- Do I ever think (as I have done some years back) of seeing myself at the top of the ladder of life?
- Am I comfortable with where I am right now?
- What do I think I can do best or reasonably well?
- Do I swim with the ocean current or against it?
- Above all, have I discovered my purpose in life?

In the book of Genesis on the account of Creation, man (Adam and Eve) was created last but was given the authority over all things first created (plants and animals alike) What an infinite-inverse paradox! The scripture also says, "God blessed them, saying to them, be fruitful, multiply, fill the earth and conquer it. Be masters of the fish of these, the bars of heaven and all living animals on the earth" (Gen. 1:26-30).

Since this is so, it's quite disturbing seeing people who have yet to discover their talents and the powers they have.

With the creation of humans, God ended the work of Creation. He left the remaining works of creation in the hands of humans. By implication, God created you and left every created thing and further works of creation in your care. By creating you, He left nothing to chance. Therefore, who you are and where you find yourself aren't by accident but by the special design of the Creator; nothing in your life is arbitrary in any way; rather, it is all for a purpose.

Since I am interested in helping you discover your purpose in life, you may consider following these steps:

- Keep your target in sight
- Have an action plan
- Challenge your excuses
- Be intentional
- Set deadlines

To put away aimlessness, purposelessness, and weakness and to begin to think purposefully is to enter the ranks of those strong ones who only recognize failure as one of the pathways to the attainment of goals, who make all conditions serve them, and who think strongly, attempt fearlessly, and accomplish masterfully, as James Allen would say. Above all else, begin to think of taking risks.

Created for a Purpose, on a Purpose

Elizabeth Kubler-Ross once said, "Learn to get in touch with the silence within yourself and know that everything in life has a purpose." In line with that, I can recall vividly during my undergraduate studies (specifically during orientation), we were tasked to answer one question. It might sound simple but requires care. The simple but difficult question was "Why am I here?" If you (as I have done) can figure out the answer to that question, you will do anything to avoid "sidetracks," that is, distractions.

Identifying, acknowledging, and honoring our life's purpose is perhaps the most important action successful people take. They take the time to understand what they are here on this earth to do, and then they pursue that with passion and enthusiasm. Thomas Edison said, "If we did all the things we're capable of, we would literally astound ourselves." Unless you have discovered something worth dying for, life may be purposeless for you. It's only when these men discover their life purpose that they spend their lives sharpening it. Take a look at these people:

- Bill Gates spent his time discovering Microsoft
- Steve Jobs discovered the Apple computer
- Thomas Edison founded General Electric
- Mark Zuckerberg developed Facebook
- Brin Sergey founded Google
- Elon Musk (co-founder of Tesla) proved the possibility of electric cars

Unless you've discovered your life's purpose (mission, if you prefer to call it that), living might seem boring and burdensome. You may ask yourself: can I identify my purpose on planet earth? To answer the question is to discover that you're created for a purpose. The scripture was quite clear that humans were created for a purpose. If we were created "for a purpose" then what about "on purpose"?

What's your purpose? Are you on a mission? To be on purpose one has to be unique and original. John Mason rightly points out that "imitation is a limitation."

A young man of fifty years once had an accident and was rushed to the hospital but, during a major operation, he died in the theatre. Reaching heaven, God told him to go back, that it wasn't yet his time to die and that he had fifty years more to live. At the sound of this, he became happy and returned to life. After his discharge from the hospital, he went to a beauty clinic and worked on his skin, changed the color of his hair, and said to himself, "Since I still have fifty more years to live, I'm going to make great use of this opportunity."

Soon after, while crossing the road, out of excitement, he failed to look carefully and was hit by a car and this time, he died on the spot. Getting to God, he furiously asked, "Why should you allow that car to kill me? Weren't you the one that told me that I had more fifty years to live on earth the first time I died and came to you? Why should you do this thing after I've spent a huge amount of money in the beauty clinic to clean up and beautify myself? This is unfair."

After his complaints, God looked at him and uttered, "Actually, my son, I told you that you will live more fifty years and I was fully ready to protect you. But, as you went to change your skin, color of your hair, and some of your features, I no longer recognized you, and that was why the car was able to hit and kill you. If you hadn't changed yourself to look like another person, I would have recognized you and prevented you from any harm."

This story points to the fact that you might end in pain, failure, backwardness, frustration, misery, regrets, and untimely death if you refuse to be you. It depicts what may happen if you fail to discover your life's purpose and dwell on it. No wonder Russell Kelfer, in one of his poems, writes that "You're who you're for a reason. You're part of an intricate plan. You're a precious and perfect unique design, called God's special woman or man."

Similarly, John Mason speaks plainly that "there's only one life for you – your own. The person who walks in someone else's tracks never leaves his own footprint." An African proverb sheds more insight by saying "No matter how long a wood remains in the water, it will never become a crocodile." And the Bible summarizes this unchangeable nature of inherent characteristics by saying "Can the Ethiopian change his skin or the leopard his spots?" (Jer. 13:23).

As a way to help you live a purposeful life, let's consider what Robert Kiyosaki called the "Eight integrities of a business." According to him, for any entrepreneur to be successful, they must have a sense of mission, which acts as a pillar to a castle. Mission (purpose) is the spiritual reason for the existence of the business. For instance, the first lesson someone admitted to the military receives is on the importance of a mission. Also, in religion, missionaries have a mission and focus on it. To be "on purpose" means you're doing what you love to do; doing what you're good at and accomplishing what's important to you.

The good news is that when you truly are "on purpose," the people, resources, and opportunities you need naturally gravitate toward you. Some time ago, during Christmas, I had a chat with one of my family friends, Olivia. She said something that was amazing: "Well, one thing that I like doing is to put just a little smile on people's faces." Always remember that if you can't do a great thing, you can do a small thing in a big way.

Breakdown for a Breakthrough

Felix A. O. McDon's, in *You Can Rise to the Top*, made a beautiful statement: "I once saw a banner on my street advertising a church program, and the inscription on it went thus: 'say goodbye to failure.'" For McDon, when he saw it, he felt uncomfortable because the message of such inscriptions makes people feel that they can become successful by coming to the crusade. But is it so?

I don't intend to sound ascetical or religious here. So, please, I ask your pardon if you see it either way. I am an Igbo man, and I am humbled about my ancestral heritage. One of the things an Igbo man likes to do is speak in proverbs and make analogies. So, permit me to make an analogy. Has it ever crossed your mind how a little seed, such as maize, okra, acorn, or any vegetable, will grow to become beneficial and nutritional to us? What's the magic, in other words, the secret behind it that after planting, the small seed of maize or corn will grow to become multiple seeds – while also maturing to be a plant? The secret (or magic, if you prefer) is that it must break down for there to be a breakthrough.

The scriptural text affirms that "Unless a seed falls to the soil and dies, it remains only a single seed" (Jn. 12:24-25). For the maize seed to bring out its lovely bunch of seeds, it must decay (break down) and acquire the necessary nutrients – new nutrients from the soil to germinate and mature as adult maize ready for consumption. Those processes that it goes through are what you, the reader, need to scale through to the ladder of success.

Many people are where they are today just because they don't want to break down to breakthrough; in other words, they don't want to give away or let go of their old doctrines of life for a better view of it.

An Igbo adage says, "You can't have a complete and better view of a masquerade dance from a particular standpoint." This means that one has to make a little adjustment – a paradigm shift (culturally, tradition-ally, religiously, and politically) in order for the superior versions of them to evolve. But this doesn't mean the abandonment of the "old self" com-pletely. For a person to get to a new destination, it requires movement and a change in lifestyle, goal, and motivation. Thus, for a breakdown to have a breakthrough, I recommend the following exercises:

- Have a list of goals you intend to achieve
- Set a deadline
- Create a diary of goals
- Write your goals out in detail
- Reread your goals daily
- Carry your most important goal in your wallet

Have a list of goals you intend to achieve

Napoleon Hill once said that "there's one quality which one must possess to win, and that's definiteness of purpose, the knowledge of what one wants, and a burning desire to possess it." Once you know your life's purpose, determine your vision, and clarify what your true needs and desires are, you have to convert them into specific, measurable goals and objectives and then act on them with Rene Descartes' certainty that you will achieve them. Because of the organogenesis (the make-up) of the brain, experts are of the view that whatever goal you give to your subconscious mind it will work night and day to achieve.

In setting your goals, I advise you don't go for cheap ones you can ride over within the twinkling of an eye; rather, go for goals that stretch and challenge you. Andrew Carnegie said, "If you want to be happy, set a goal that commands your thoughts, liberates your energy, and inspires your hopes."

Set a deadline

For a breakthrough, you need to set a deadline. Before I start working on a goal (like authoring this book), I set the completion date and time. To make sure the goal unleashes the power of your subconscious mind, it must meet two criteria: how much and when. For instance, you could measure it by saying 135 pounds by 5:00 p.m. on June 30, 2024. Always remember that vague goals produce vague results.

Create a diary

It's not enough to write down your goals; you need a separate goal book. Some people would prefer to write their goals on a 3×5 index card, which would be easy to carry everywhere you go, even when you travel. This is another powerful way to speed up the achievement of your goals. Buy a three-ring binder, a scrapbook, or a journal then create a separate page for each of your goals. Write the goal at the top of the page and then illustrate it with pictures, words, and phrases you cut out of magazines, catalogues, and brochures that depict your goal as already achieved.

Write your goals out in detail

To differentiate a goal from a good idea, it's important to write out your proposed goals in detail. One of the best ways to get clarity and specificity is to write them out as if you're writing items to be purchased from the market. When you do this, your subconscious mind will know what to work on. It will know which opportunities to explore to help you reach your goal. As a one-time editor-in-chief of my university's magazine, I followed this guideline when we were preparing for publication, and it was a success.

Reread your goals daily

Having written down your goals in detail, activate the powers of your subconscious mind by reviewing your list. Experts like Jack Canfield suggest two or three times every day, first thing after waking up and last thing before going to sleep. Close your eyes and picture each goal as if it were already accomplished. Doing this increases what psychologists call the "structural tension" in your brain.

Carry your most important goal in your wallet

When Olympic decathlon gold medalist Bruce Jenner asked a roomful of Olympic hopefuls if they had a list of written goals, everyone raised their hands. When he asked how many of them had that list with them right that moment, only one person raised their hand. That person was Dan O'Brien, who went on to win the gold medal in the decathlon at the 1996 Olympics in Atlanta.

Jack Canfield, while working for W. Clement Stone, gave him the idea of carrying his most important goal in his wallet. In addition, also keep an index pack or notepad in your pocket to note down your "hunches."

One goal isn't enough

Lou Holtz (the only coach in NCAA history to ever lead six different college teams to post-season bowl games) once said, "If you are bored with life, if you don't get up every morning with a burning desire to do things, you don't have enough goals." You must get off your bottom if you want to get to the top of your goals. Holtz is a goal-setter who learned his lesson after reading *The Magic of Thinking Big* by David Schwartz.

Authoring a book has always been one of my goals. So, now that it has been achieved, victory has been inscribed next to it in my goal book. Now, what about you? Why don't you try the breakdown for a breakthrough?

See What You Want, Get What You See

Let's call this imagination. The power of imagination is, in my view, a "wonder-work." Albert Einstein (winner of the Nobel Prize for Physics) once said that "imagination is everything. It's the preview of life's coming attraction." As a person strives toward the ladder of success, he has to imbibe the act of imagination (visualization, if you prefer to call it). This single act of visualization/imagination (the act of creating compelling and vivid pictures in your mind) may be the most underutilized tool you possess because it greatly accelerates success in three powerful ways:

1. It activates the creative powers of your subconscious mind.
2. It focuses your brain by programming its reticular activating system (RAS) to notice available resources that were always there but were previously unnoticed.
3. It magnetizes and attracts to you the people, resources, and opportunities you need to achieve your goal.

A research project at Harvard University found that students who visualized in advance performed tasks with nearly 100% accuracy, whereas students who didn't visualize achieved only 55% accuracy. My friend Solomon advised me some time ago to always indulge in imagination. For him, nine out of ten people fail to succeed because they don't visualize their "tomorrows." This simple act puts you one step ahead of others.

The legendary golfer Jack Nicklaus describes how he always visualize his shots with great detail before executing them, imagining where he wants the ball to end up and how it will get there. This mental process helps him prepare for his swings and turns his visualizations into reality on the golf course.

The power of imagination has done great work in the lives of the ancient sages. "To do much clear thinking," said Thomas A. Edison, "a man must arrange for a regular period of solitude when he can concentrate and indulge his imagination without distraction."

A Kurdish proverb says, "Solitude is the nest of thought."

"I have never found a companion that was so companionable as solitude," says Henry David Thoreau.

You can imagine how much solitude I must have experienced authoring this book.

Hold on. What kind of imagination am I talking about here? Paraphrasing the explanation of Dr. Sydney Newton Bremer from *How to Get What You Want*, there are two types of imagination: **Reproductive** and **Creative**. The former is the mental action of reproducing mental images stored in the memory under the suggestion of associated images. In this matter, we are able to revisit places we have been in times past. This type of imagination is indulged in by students (during the revision period in preparation for classroom exams) in order to have excellent grades. I like to call this type "the imagination of what is."

The latter is the process of combining former experiences in the creation of new images that are different from any of those previously experienced. It's this type of imagination that has benefited mankind and left its mark upon the world through inventions and discoveries since the dawn of civilization. In my view, this imagination is what should be used. It is creative imagination that:

- Led Orville and Wilbur Wright to the invention of the airplane.
- Triggered Alexander Graham Bell to invent the telephone.
- Spurred Christopher Columbus to discover America.
- Moved Llyod M. Smith to invent the DNA sequencer.
- Energized John Logie Baird (television), Marconi (radio), Auguste and Louis Lumiere (cinema), Thomas Alva Edison (film projection system), L.J.M. Dauguerre and J.N. Neipce (photography), Steve Jobs (Apple computer), Mark Zuckerberg (Facebook), Philip Emeagwali (Internet), Sergey Brin (Google), and Bill Gates (Microsoft) to proceed with their respective inventions.

Just in science alone, creative imagination has engineered "men of theoria" like Socrates, Plato, Saint Augustine, and Thomas Aquinas to propound their philosophies and theologies. For instance, Socrates once said, "Man, know thyself; for an unexamined life isn't worth living." Taking it a step further, Plato said "Unless philosophers become kings, and kings become philosophers, there will never be peace in the State." One of the famous quotations of Machiavelli is, "For a prince to rule well, he must be a man and a beast."

The same imagination could have spurred Dr. Martin Luther King to prophesy, "I have a dream . . . "

Knowing this, the questions we may be battling with include:

- How does visualization work?
- What's the process for visioning?
- What if I don't "see" anything when I visualize?

Don't work yourself up if you can't find answers to the questions. I will journey with you to figure it out.

How does visualization work?

One of my favorite quotes from the Greek philosopher Socrates is "Virtue is knowledge. Since knowledge is teachable, virtue is also teachable." That maxim should be a great consolation for us. Always remember that people often criticize and fear what they don't understand or are not familiar with. Also, keep in mind that ignorance can lead to negative judgements and apprehension toward unfamiliar concepts or experience. So, resist the urge to critique what you are not too familiar with.

When you visualize your goals every day, it creates a conflict in your subconscious mind between what you're visualizing and what you currently have. Your subconscious mind tries to resolve that conflict by turning your current reality into a new, more exciting vision. When this conflict is intensified over a long period, it causes three things to happen:

1. It programs your brain's RAS to start letting into your awareness anything that will help you achieve your goals.

2. It activates your subconscious mind to create solutions for getting the goals you want.

3. It creates new levels of motivation, that is, unexpectedly doing things that take you to your goals.

What's the process for visualizing?

This is quite a simple one. All that is involved is for you to close your eyes and "see" your goals as already complete. The whole process will take between ten and fifteen minutes, depending on how many goals you have. If you meditate, does your visualization sharpen after you finish meditating? The deepened state you have achieved in meditation will heighten the impact of your visualization.

To multiply the effect many times over, add sounds, smells, tastes, and feelings to your pictures. In fact, start acting as if your goals are already achieved.

What if I don't "see" anything when I visualize?

Jack Canfield said that "most people are eidetic visualizers; when they close their eyes, they see everything in bright, clear, three-dimensional technicolor images." If you're non-eidetic, I suggest you use printed pictures in your visualization process. For example, if one of your goals is to own a new Lexus LS-430, you can take your camera down to your local Lexus dealer and ask a salesperson to take a picture of you sitting behind the wheel. Also, if your goal is to be a millionaire, you might want to write yourself a check or create a bank statement that shows your bank account.

Once you have created these images, you can place them (one to a page) in a three-ring binder that you review every day. Or you can place it on a refrigerator door, somewhere where you will see it every day.

Break it Down; Release the Brake

Mark Twain said, "The secret of getting ahead is getting started. The secret of getting started is breaking your complex, overwhelming tasks into small manageable tasks, and then starting on the first one."

Read that one more time and let it convey a message to you. The next step is to determine all the individual actions you will need to take to accomplish your goal(s).

How do you piece the goals together? If you can't identify it now, don't worry. There are several ways to figure out the actions you will need to take to accomplish your goals. They include the following:

- Consult with people who have already done what you want to do and ask them about the steps they took.
- Purchase a book or manual that outlines the process.
- Use mind-mapping.
- Make a daily to-do list.
- Plan your day the night before.
- Use AFS – "Achievers Focusing System."

Consult with people who have already done what you want to do:

Anthony Robbins said that "success leaves clues." When I was growing up, I heard "nothing is new under the sun," but it was unclear to me what that meant. My interpretation of that has been that there's nothing you are trying to do that has never been done by somebody, somewhere, sometime.

One of the great things about living in today's world of abundance and opportunity is that almost everything you want to do has already been done by someone else, whether it's losing weight, running a marathon, starting a business, writing a musical composition, becoming financially independent, etcetera. Someone has already done it and left clues in the form of books, manuals, audio and video programs, workshops, you name it.

For instance, if you want to be financially independent, there are hundreds of books, ranging from *Multiple Streams of Income* by Robert G.

Allen to *Rich Dad Poor Dad* by Robert T. Kiyosaki. If you want to have a better relationship with your spouse, you can read John Gray's *Men Are from Mars, Women Are from Venus.* When you take advantage of information, you will discover that life is simply a connect-the-dots game, as Jack Canfield would say, and all the dots have already been identified and organized by somebody else. All you have to do is follow the blueprint and get started.

Not everybody can seek the already laid-down blueprint. Many people aren't concerned about seeking success clues. Here are some reasons why:

- It never occurs to us since we never see others doing it (such as friends or parents).
- It is inconvenient.
- We are afraid to take a risk and fear rejection.
- Connecting the dots in a new way would mean change (which is uncomfortable).
- Connecting the dots means hard work, which most people won't indulge in.

To what extent do you think those highlighted points are true? Here are three ways you can begin to seek out clues:

1. Seek out a teacher, coach, mentor, manual, or an audio program on the internet to help you achieve your major goals.
2. Seek out someone who has already done what you want to do (ask them for an interview).
3. Ask someone if you can shadow them for a day and watch them work.

Purchase a book or manual that outlines the process:

There are a myriad of books that contain valuable information on what you want to achieve. When I was drafting this book, I enjoyed reading *Goals* by Brian Tracy.

Use mind-mapping:

This means brainstorming or strategizing with many people on how to give victory to your dream goals. It is a simple but powerful process of creating a detailed to-do list for achieving your goal, including information you will need to gather, who you will need to talk to, what small steps you will need to take, how much money you will need to earn/raise, which deadlines you will need to meet, etcetera.

Make a daily to-do list

Talk is cheap, and nothing works until you work on it. Thus, once you have completed a mind- mapping for your goal, convert all the to-do items into daily actions, listing each one and committing it to completion, adding date for each one.

After making your to-do list, do the first thing first. This is a fight against procrastination. Brian Tracy wrote about this in *Eat That Frog! 21 Great Ways to Stop Procrastinating and Get More Done in Less Time.* Brian recommends goal setters identify the five things they must accomplish on any given day, and then pick the one they absolutely must do first. This becomes your biggest and ugliest frog. He suggests you accomplish that task first; in essence, eat that frog first.

Plan your day the night before:

One of the places you could see this exercise in action is in a religious educational setting, where activities are planned ahead of time. One of the most powerful tools high-achievers use for breaking things down, gaining control over their life, and increasing their productivity is to plan their next day the night before. There are two major reasons (at least based on experience):

1. If you plan your day the night before, your subconscious mind will work on these tasks all night long, which enables you to think of creative ways to solve problems, overcome obstacles, and achieve your desired outcomes.

2. By creating your to-do list the night before, you can start your day running. This implies you know exactly what you are going to do and in what order, which helps you to pull together any materials you need.

Use AFS:

A valuable tool that will really keep you focused on achieving all your goals is AFS, which stands for Achievers Focusing System. This was developed by Les Hewitt of the Achievers Coaching Program. To get more information on this, check this link: www.thesuccessprinciples.com.

Develop Your Own Success Formula

I would like to pick on your brain at this point, so stay with me on this one. One of the ways to help a student is using the "Socratic method" of questioning and answering.

You may agree or disagree with me on some of the things I will highlight here. I only intend to act as a "gadfly," as Plato described in the *Apology*, helping you to discover the best in yourself. Abundance can only come to an optimistic, sufficient, and trustful mind.

One of the major reasons the lower class and even the middle class criticize and condemn the rich most of the time is their inability to know and understand success principles or secrets. Just as any society, government, culture, or organization has rules, regulations, and laws guiding them for the purpose of achieving their goals, so also it is necessary that people do this in order to attain their goals.

By looking at several works of literature and also the Bible, I realize that there are a series of success formulas. These formulas may serve as shortcuts to the attainment of goals. Based on my scriptural discovery, I summarize the success formula in the Bible as the philosophy of Jesus Christ. The scripture says:

> . . . and they said to him, what authority have you for acting like this? Jesus said to them, I'll tell you my authority for acting like this: John's baptism, did it come from

heaven or from man? Answer that – So the reply to Jesus was: we don't know. And Jesus said to them, nor will I tell you my authority for acting like this (Mk.11:27-33).

It doesn't just stop there.

Most of the books I have read and audio tapes I have listened to have one thing in common – a promise for both young and old. Most prolific writers are on the move to unleash the success formulas. Sometimes it might be overwhelming to assimilate the information. Most, if not all, suggest you get out of your comfort zones. Some recommendations on books that could help you as you get your life's bearing include:

- Robin Sharma's *LWT*
- Greg Reid's *Three Feet from Gold*
- Robert T. Kiyosaki's *CashFlow Quadrant*

Robin Sharma's LWT:

Robin, in *The Leader Who Had No Title,* outlines some of these success formulas that may be beneficial to you as a reader. I have tried to summarize them in a nutshell for your easy digestion. They include:

LWT = *L*eader *W*ithout *T*itle

IMAGE = *I*nnovation *M*astery *A*uthenticity *G*uts and *E*thics

Let's look at them, starting with LWT = a Leader Without Title. The first thing you should consider is the accumulation of titles so as to attract attention, respect, and honor. An LWT is one who goes to bed late but rises early because they believe that it is fine to be content but not to be satisfied.

The second formula talks about **IMAGE**. Because we live in what Sharma calls a "Remake Nation," innovation always trumps repeating what might have worked in the past. It is simply making this day better than yesterday, thereby "living in the day-tight compartment." The "M," which stands for **Mastery** suggests committing yourself to mastery of what you do, mastery of your craft, which is the only standard to operate in these change-rich times. To summarize Mastery, Steve Martin (a comedian) says that it is to "be so good that people can't ignore you." The "A" from IMAGE stands for **Authenticity**. Goal attainment is all about closing your ears to the noisy voices of others so you can more clearly hear the mission and call within yourself. This reminds me of the words of Dr. Seuss and Michael Jordan, respectively. Dr. Seuss is of the view that you should "be who you are and say what you feel because those who mind don't matter and those who matter don't mind." The legendary basketball player Michael Jordan, in his book *Driven from Within*, once said that "authority is about being true to who you are even when everyone around you wants you to be someone else."

The "G" simply stands for the need to have **Guts**. For you to make your marks, you need to be tough and have big guts. You will need to dare more than the reasonable person and risk far more than the ordinary person.

Lastly, the "E" stands for **Ethics**. This is the word that's mostly forgotten by everyone in this topsy-turvy society. Sadly enough, people cut corners; they prefer the cash grab, thinking only about themselves, but you can only get whatever you want in life faster by always help others to get whatever they want first.

Greg Reid's Three Feet from Gold:

Oliver Wendell Holmes opines that "a mind once exposed to a new idea never regains its original dimensions." In writing the book *The Feet from Gold*, Greg employed the principles of success he learned from the entrepreneurs he had interviewed. His journey was a true example of the principle **Never Give Up**. The success equation/formula he proposed was: $[(P+T) \times A \times A] + F = $ Your Success.

The above formula simply means combine *P*assion (something that makes your heart sing) with *T*alent (something you excel in), multiply it by the right *A*ssociation (successful people or organizations), and *A*ction (concrete steps you can take toward your goal), and then add your *F*aith (the unwavering belief in yourself), and you will have your success. I have tried it and it worked and has continued to work for me.

Robert T. Kiyosaki's CashFlow Quadrant:

The majority of the less financially privileged people learned things (especially innovative ideas) the hard way. In his *New York Times* and The *Wall Street Journal* bestselling book *Rich Dad Poor Dad*, Robert T. Kiyosaki talks about how he learned the "rules of money" from his rich dad. One of the greatest ideas (at least for me) was that "the rich don't work for money; rather money works for them." Do you work for money or does money work for you?

I recommend you read more on his *The CashFlow Quadrant*. The simple information he offers is that each person is either an employee, self-employed, in business, or an investor. These four different types of people make up the world of business, and it explores who they are and what makes individuals in each quadrant unique. Employees and self-employed individuals (those who work for money) reside on the left side of the quadrant, while the right side of the quadrant is for individuals who receive their cash from the business or investments they own (those whom money works for).

In all these success formulas, the most important single ingredient is knowing how to get along with people. I would like to know: have you used any of these success formulas? Do you think it's something worth trying?

Takeaway from Chapter Two

► It's quite unfortunate that a lot of people do not know where they're coming from, where they're going, or what they want out of their lives. The first secret of success is to know your *Definite Chief Aim* –**DCA**.

► Human beings (Adam and Eve) were created last, according to biblical injunction, and placed in charge of all other creatures, including our own selves. This shows the enormous powers of man as confessed by the Psalmist (Ps. 8:3-6).

► Are you created just for a purpose or only on purpose? Attempting an answer is for you to know that you have a share in God's creation. What impact have you made on yourself and the people around you? Be true and sincere to yourself, humanity at large, and to God.

► Are you a dogmatist? Do you stick strictly to rules that do not allow you to have a new idea about your life and the world you live in? The acceptance of new knowledge enables and empowers you to have a "breakdown so as to have a breakthrough; no new wine can be poured inside an old wine skin (Matt. 9:17)

► How often have you indulged in the power of imagination and visualization? Do you see things as they are or as they should be? The latter is the power of imagination, while the former is living today. Think and plan ahead; it keeps you two steps ahead of others.

► Successful people are willing to leave clues, but human beings are a problem unto themselves. To achieve success, look for success clues; get them from those who have already done what you intend to do.

► As you climb up the ladder of success, have your own success "Golden Key"; I encourage you to develop your own success formula.

CHAPTER THREE

If You Don't Have it, Search for it

"Iron rusts from disuse; stagnant water loses its purity
and in cold weather becomes frozen; even so does
inaction sap the vigors of the mind."

—Leonardo da Vinci

Goal-Driven

One of the sole purposes of this book is to get you to decamp from mediocrity to enlightenment. On opening the thirteenth page of Brian Tracy's *Goals: How to Get Everything You Want – Faster than You Ever Thought Possible*, something caught my attention. It's Victor Frank, the founder of logotherapy's, statement: "The greatest need of human beings is for a sense of meaning and purpose in life." In other words, he was talking about being goal driven and becoming motivated by those goals (your Definite Chief Aim).

Let me share a fictional story titled "The Treasure Island." It's about two friends named Philip and Alex. Philip is weak-willed while Alex is strong-willed. They set out differently on a journey to The Treasure Island in search of some monks who have good knowledge of nature and navigation systems. Fortunately for them, at different times, they meet an old man who gives them directions to the monks. On their meeting with the monks, they receive a map that will lead to a settlement close to The Treasure Island, occupied by an old guru. The instruction given to them is: once you see the old guru, tell him that you are going to The Treasure Island, and he will show you the way. Without much ado, they leave immediately. Just a few minutes from the monks' residence, they arrived at the old guru's house and make their intentions known.

Philip, who arrived first, asked where the road to The Treasure Island was. The old guru didn't utter a word, but instead pointed to a very narrow road – an odd place in the distance. With a heart full of joy, Philip left, but something happened. He encountered what I call "temporary defeat." First, he fell into a deep pit and then he was attacked by bees.

After encountering the bees, Alex arrived and asked for the direction. The old guru pointed in the same direction. He didn't waste a minute heading in that direction. After a brief moment, the old guru said to Philip, "The Treasure Island where lies a box of treasure is that way, just a little distance from where you were attacked by bees." Before the old guru could finish his sentence, Alex arrived with the box of treasure – yet both were sent in the same direction and encountered the same challenge.

Why is it that Philip didn't succeed in his quest while Alex did? Alex was goal-driven: he knew what he was after. He was ready to pay the price involved in his journey, but Philip thought he could get it on a platter of gold, not knowing that "nothing good comes easy." In other words, Alex was decisive and specific in his mission to The Treasure Island.

Now I ask you, have you decided what you want? What have you planned to get out of life? What do you want? To be goal-driven, I recommend three essential exercises for you:

- Decide what you want
- Train/empower the will
- Avoid procrastination

Decide what you want:

Ben Stein (actor and author) said that "the indispensable first step to getting the things you want out of life is this: decide what you want." Once you know that you are created for a purpose, and then on purpose, this permeates into your subconscious mind what you intend to achieve. For researchers like Jack Canfield, one of the main reasons why most people don't get what they want is that they haven't decided what they want; they haven't defined their desires in clear and compelling detail.

Can you remember how you got what you wanted when you were just a little kid? You started out as a baby knowing exactly what you wanted. You knew when you were hungry. You spat out the foods you didn't like and avidly devoured things you wanted. You had no trouble expressing your needs and wants. You simply cried loudly (with no inhibitions) until you got what you wanted. You had everything inside of you that you needed to get fed, changed, held, and rocked.

Making that decision now that you have grown older may be a bit difficult (but only if you allow it) because of either the fear of its consequences or choosing the wrong goal. Thus, as a guide to deciding what you want, perhaps the following ideas might help:

- Be aware of the consequences.
- Believe you can (if anybody can, you can).
- Consult past decisions (history and people).
- Think systematically and critically.
- In moments of confusion, seek advice.

Train/empower the will:

Of Julius Caesar, it was said by a contemporary that it was his activity and giant determination, rather than his military skill, that won his victories. Where there is a will, there is a way, so they say. The person who starts out in life determined to make the most of his abilities and lets nothing escape him that he can possibly use for his own advancement, who keeps his ears open for every sound that can help him on his way, who keeps his hands open that he may clutch every opportunity, who is ever on the alert for everything that can help him to get on in the world – that person will be sure to make his life successful, for where men wait for opportunities, strong men make them.

James Allen, in his work, *Mind Is the Master*, explains the empowering of the will. He wrote, "Without the strength of mind, nothing worthy of accomplishment can be done, and the cultivation of that steadfastness and stability of character which is commonly called will-power is one of the foremost duties of man, for its possession is essentially necessary both to his moral and eternal well-being." All the means for the cultivation of the will are already at hand in the mind and life of the individual; they reside in the weak side of his character, which by attacking and vanquishing the necessary strength of will, will be developed.

From research (and partly from experience), I have discovered seven rules and principles for the training or empowering of the will, which include:

1. Break off bad habits.
2. Form good habits.
3. Give scrupulous attention to the duty of the present moment.
4. Do vigorously, and at once, whatever has to be done.
5. Live by rules.
6. Control the tongue.
7. Control the mind.

I can guarantee that if you meditate upon and diligently practice these rules, you won't fail to develop that purity of purpose and power of will, which will enable you to successfully cope with every difficulty and pass triumphantly through every emergency.

Avoid procrastination:

As a way of measuring your progress to success, you have to shun procrastination. In understanding the pain of deadly weapons, Edward Young said that "the best way to get something done is to begin." Etymologically, procrastination is derived from the Latin "pro" – "in favor of," and "cras" – "tomorrow." Thus, it literally means "in favor of tomorrow."

However, psychologically, procrastination, according to Clarry Lay, "occurs when there's a temporary gap between intended behavior and enacted behavior. It happens when there's a significant duration between when people intend to do a job and when they actually do it; one of the attributes of procrastinators is talking more and less of action."

People indulge in procrastination for many reasons, some of which include:

- Lack of proper organization of priorities.
- Lack of skill.
- Lack of interest and enthusiasm.
- Lack of self-discipline.
- Perfectionism.
- Indecision.

To help you address this issue, there are strategies/techniques you could use. Because tomorrow never comes, some of the major proven methods to fight and get rid of procrastination include:

- Take immediate action.
- Be organized.
- Plan your day.
- Make it urgent.
- Plan your reward.
- Be purposeful.

The Peanut Crack; Happiness at Last

Something got my attention one day when I was reading the Bible. The meaning of a scriptural passage took some time for me to understand and digest. It's Jotham's fable and it reads:

> One day the trees went out to anoint a king to rule over them. They said to the olive tree, be our king! The olive tree answered them: must I forego my oil which gives honor to gods and men, to stand swaying above the trees? Then the trees said to the fig trees: come now, you be our king! The fig tree answered them, must I forego my sweetness, forego my excellent fruit, to stand swaying above the trees? Then all the trees said to the thorn bush: come now,

you be our king! And the thorn bush answered the trees:
if in all good faith you anoint me king to reign over you,
then come and shelter in my shade (Jg. 9:715).

One thing is certain: every success requires some amount of sacrifice. What does the story tell you? Put differently, what is the takeaway from the story? Out of curiosity, have you ever entertained the thought that success comes on a platter of gold? From when I was a little boy till now, I have heard "no cross, no crown" or "nothing good comes easy" many times.

According to the Bible, Jesus Christ came to the world to save humanity from sin. But, for Him to enter into His glory, He had to experience some necessary obstacles and suffering. At some point it became unbearable for Him, and he made a plea as seen in (Matt. 26:38-39; Mk. 14:34-36; Lk. 22:42-44): "My father, if it's possible, let this cup pass me by. Nevertheless, let it be as you, not I, would have it."

For people who are goal driven, to enter into your own glory, you must have your own peanut to crack, and that is experiencing the roadblock, which is the springboard to success. For great men like Nelson Mandela, Martin Luther, and many others (who have left a legacy), it was not easy to enter their glory. Even in the Christians' book of worship, it was not easy for the seven brothers to experience martyrdom for them to enter their glory (2 Mac. 7:1-43).

If you have a problem, that's good! Obstacles are not bad in and of them-selves. It's not evil to experience problems (it does not necessarily indicate moral wrongdoing or evilness – it could be an opportunity for growth) because repeated victories over your problems are the rungs on your ladder of success. But then, with each victory, you grow in wisdom, stature, and experience. In fact, when you become a better, bigger, more successful person, each time you meet a problem, try to tackle and conquer it with "PMA – Positive Mental Attitude," as Napoleon Hill suggests in *Think and Grow Rich*.

Everyone has problems. This is because you and everything in the uni-verse are in a constant process of change (an inexorable natural law). What's important to you is that your success or failure to meet the challenges of change is dependent upon your mental attitude. Somebody ascribed this organization as a "Mentality Change Organization."

James Allen would say that dispersion is weakness; concentration is purpose. Destruction is a scattering; preservation a uniting process. Things are useful and thoughts are powerful in the measure that their parts are strongly and intelligently concentrated. Purpose is a highly concentrated thought. All the mental energies are directed to the attainment of an objective, and obstacles that intervene between the thinker and the objective are, one after another, broken down and overcome. Empty whims, ephemeral fancies, vague desires, and half-hearted resolutions have no place in purpose.

How does a person meet a problem with PMA? Relying on the first principal element and premise that God is always a good God, I would strongly recommend you attempt the following formulas put together here from experience and research:

- Ask for divine guidance in finding the right solution.
- Engage in thinking time to solve core problems. Remember that every adversity has the seed of an equivalent or greater benefit for those who have PMA.
- State the problem; analyze and define it.
- Say to yourself enthusiastically: "That's good!"
- Ask yourself specific questions, such as: What's good about it? How can I turn this adversity into a seed of equivalent or greater benefit?
- Keep searching for answers to these questions until you find at least one answer that can work.

While you go through the exercise, you might be wondering if there is happiness at last. The Bible (and other religious books of worship, I believe) are filled with promises that there is a silver lining above the sky. For instance, the Psalmist says, "those who are sowing in tears will sing when they reap" (Ps. 126:5). The Bible further says, "There is a season for everything: a time for every occupation under heaven" (Ecc. 3:1-8). Joy is always the accompaniment of a task successfully accomplished. An undertaking completed, or a piece of work done, always brings test and satisfaction. "When a man has done his duty, he's light-hearted and happy," says Emerson. However insignificant the task may appear, doing it faithfully and with the whole soul energy always results in cheerfulness and peace of mind.

How happy is a child when a school lesson, long labored over, is mastered at last? The athlete, who has trained his body through long months or years of discipline and strain, is richly blessed in his increased health and strength and is met with the rejoicing of his friends when he carries home the prize from the field of contest. After many years of ungrudging toil, the heart of the scholar is gladdened with the advantages and power that learning bestows. The businessman, grappling incessantly with difficulties and drawbacks, is amply repaid in the happy assurance of well-earned success, and the horticulturist, vigorously contending with the stubborn soil, sits down at last to eat of the fruits of his labor.

According to James Allen, every successful accomplishment, even in worldly things, is repaid with its own measure of joy, and in spiritual things, the joy that supervenes upon the perfection of purpose is sure, deep, and abiding. Great is the heartfelt joy when, after innumerable and apparently unsuccessful attempts, some ingrained fault of character is at last cut out, to trouble its erstwhile victim and the world no more. The striver after virtue (he who is engaged in the holy task of building up a noble character) tastes at every step of conquest over self a joy that doesn't again leave him, but which becomes an integral part of his spiritual nature. In everything you do, pay now to play later on!

The Mentor and the Mentee

How would you understand it when I say that "a candle loses none of its light by lighting another candle?" What if "no one loses anything by teaching his fellow?" In influencing others, Henry Brooke Adams writes, "A teacher affects eternity; he can never tell where his influence stops."

Imagine a football team without a coach; so is life without an influencer – particularly a mentor. This act of mentorship has been tagged with different names in different areas of life. For instance, in politics, it's called "godfather," while in the religious or Christian circle, it's called "spiritual director/advisor." Some call it a "role model." All other areas of life have their own tag names, but their centrifugal meaning lies in the influence of someone's life on another person.

The scripture made mention of Jesus Christ once saying, "I and my father are one; and that whatever I have known, I have gotten/learned from my father" (Jn.17:10-14, 22-23). From my viewpoint, it simply means (literally, not theologically) that God the Father has a great influence in the life of God the Son. You may recall the narrative between these great OT (Old Testament) prophets. Elijah mentored Elisha as seen in (2 Kg. 2:1-18).

One of my favorite statements by Ben Carson is "there's no such person as a self-made individual." In his bestselling book *Think Big*, he told the story of his mentors, inspirers, and influencers. His statement is true because I have experienced it, and many great world achievers would concur with me. For Carson, his mentors are those unique individuals who saw potential in him long before he perceived it himself; people who challenged him to do more, even when they didn't realize that they were challenging him and guiding him toward excellence. Carson wouldn't complete his life story without mentioning the four outstanding influencers in his life: William Jaeck (fifth-grade science teacher), Frank McCotter (high school biology teacher), Lemuel Doakes (band director), and Aubery Tompkins (choir director). More of his story can be found in the *Gifted Hands: The Ben Carson Story*.

Not only Carson, but every great or famous people has their mentors, inspirers, and influencers. Some of these include:

- Robert T. Kiyosaki has mentors he called the Rich Dad and the Poor Dad.
- Napoleon Hill had his influence and inspiration from Andrew Carnegie.
- Jack Canfield has his mentor/influencer known as W. Clement Stone.
- In *The Leader Who Had No Title*, Blake Dais had a mentor, Tommy Flinn.
- Rev. Fr. Ejike Mbaka (an influential religious leader in Nigeria) has his mentor, spiritual advisor, and director, Rev. Fr. Stephen Njoku.

I have my own mentors, inspirers, and influencers that I have grouped into two categories: school and home mentors. While school mentors have assisted in directing my attention to acquiring life's tools (academic and skill-related), home mentors have helped and continued to provide me with personal guidance on soft skills.

Mac Ginis rightly pointed out that there's no more noble occupation in the world than to assist someone to succeed. It is the greatest gift a human being could offer others. To better explain this mentorship, let me use the analogy of vegetables. While growing, if left unattended by the farmer, the food will rot on the ground.

According to history, it was Homer's *Odyssey* that first gave rise to the term "mentor" through the character called Mentor, who, even though he was presented as a somewhat debilitated old man, was actually used by Athena, the goddess of wisdom, to guide Odysseus's son, Telemachus, through a difficult time in the young man's life.

In ancient Greek philosophy, there were many famous mentor-mentee relationships, as can be found in the trio Socrates, Plato, and Aristotle (three great minds in philosophy who preceded each other). Socrates was a mentor to Plato, who in turn was one to Aristotle. To Alexander the Great, Aristotle was a mentor.

Continuing further, the concept of mentorship has taken various forms in different cultures and periods in history. For example, for the ancient Greeks, we find it in the concept of Pederasty (in which teachers could guide young men to greatness). The Hindu and Buddhist religions have the concept of a guru (where a wise religious person serves as the spiritual guide of someone who is misguided or who needs to know the truth). In Judaism and Christianity, we know of Jesus and his disciples/apostles (the mentor and the mentees), and Paul and Barnabas, or other times Paul and Timothy or Titus (the mentor mentoring the mentee).

The idea of mentorship is quite distinct and different from the allied force Master-Minders, which I will explain in a later chapter. Mentorship doesn't mean that the mentee should follow the mentor sheepishly or become a machine whose action is controlled by a remote; rather, it's meant to help the mentee work on specific areas for improvement to strengthen his will and to encourage hard work, personal development, and creativity.

One of my school mentors once told me, "My number-one priority is to help you become independent so as to be original in creativity."

To help you find the right mentor (or allied force), here are some highlights of characteristics a mentor should possess:

- Someone who is powerful, with a wealth of experience, since we become like those we associate with.

- Someone in your area of interest who has a good reputation.

- A person who has goodwill and is willing to assist you unconditionally.

- An individual who has significant success and is near the peak of their career.

- Someone who wins admiration easily and whom people value and respect. They should also be very motivating.

A critical component of the mentor-mentee relationship is the ability of the mentor to help the mentee to set goals for the targeted areas of improvement. However, based on my knowledge, experience, and research, some of the core functions of the mentor include:

- Ensure that the mentee's goals are specific.
- Make sure that the mentee sets goals that are realistic and attainable in a specific time frame.
- Encourage the mentee to aim for the apex while considering the priority order of the goals being set.
- Aid the mentee to set a date or goal date.
- Clarify what the mentee doesn't know.
- Choose a means to measure the mentee's progress toward each sub-goal and overall goal.
- Spur them to action.
- Teach them to be self-reliant.

While the mentee gains from the wisdom, knowledge, and experience of the mentor, the mentor gains a great deal of satisfaction from helping another person achieve their potential. Zig Ziglar summarized this when he said that "to achieve things, help others achieve their success, firstly."

Note for a mentee to keep at the back of the mind: mentors are interested in what I call PIO: Pass It On. In other words, they are willing to pass on their knowledge if you politely ask for it.

Failure Today, Success Tomorrow

I vividly recall the words of Robert G. Allen, author of *Multiple Streams of Income: How to Generate a Lifetime of Unlimited Wealth,* who once said that "everything you want is just outside your comfort zone." Think of your comfort zone as a prison you live in, which consists of the collection of "can't," "must nots," and other unfounded beliefs formed from the negative thoughts and decisions you have accumulated and reinforced during your lifetime. Perhaps you have even been trained to limit yourself.

Your comfort zone can be ascribed to a story told of a baby elephant trained at birth to be confined to a very small space. Its trainer tied its leg with a rope to a wooden post planted deep in the ground, thereby confining it to an area determined by the length of the rope. Though the baby elephant has several times tried to break the rope, it was all to no avail. Because of the number of unsuccessful attempts, it learned that it would have to stay in the area defined by the length of the rope. This continued till the elephant grew up to a size (probably a five-ton colossus) that could easily break the same rope, but it didn't even try because it learned as a baby that it couldn't break the rope. Any time I read and/or hear of this story, I always say to myself, "Poor elephant; what a low mind."

However, if this analogy describes you, the good thing is that you can change your comfort zone. The question is: how? Research shows three different ways you could do that:

1. You can use affirmations and positive self-talk to affirm already having what you want, doing what you want, and being the way you want.

2. You can create powerful and compelling new internal images of having and doing what you want.

3. You can simply change your behavior.

If we did all the things we are capable of, we would literally astound ourselves. Notice the difference between what happens when a person says to himself, "I have failed three times" and what happens when he says, "I'm a failure." S.I. Hayakawa (as quoted by S. Devaraj) says there's a world of difference between the two statements. He who says, "I have failed three times" says so just to find out why he has failed, what useful lessons he can learn from those failures, and what active steps he can take to avoid those failures in the future and achieve success in all his efforts and endeavors.

But he who says "I'm a failure" says so because he has very low self-esteem. With those words he begins to curse himself and dig his own grave. He virtually throws into the dustbin his own present and future chances of achieving success. He shuts his doors to the infinite possibilities of proving what he's capable of, what he's proficient in, and what he's gifted with. Samuel Beckett succinctly said, "Try again, fail again, fall better."

Thomas Edison (inventor of the light bulb and founder of General Electric) once said, "I haven't failed; I have found 10,000 ways that don't work." This famous American inventor summarized why so many people dare not take a bold step toward the actualization of their goals. People are afraid to fail. They are ashamed to be identified as a "failure."

I tell you most solemnly, you have not failed, and you aren't a failure until you admit that you are. Simply put, most people fail to become successful because they fail to fail enough. And in the view of Robert T. Kiyosaki in *CashFlow Quadrant,* as I explained previously, failure is one of the things that distinguishes people on the left side of the quadrant from people on the right.

What success is could vary. Success in the world of the classroom is quite distinct from success in all other spheres of life. For example, success in the world of the classroom means not making mistakes. When your report card is perfect, you get an A+. But this isn't obtainable in other areas like business. To be successful in the world of business (in the B-Business and I-Investor's quadrant, if I may borrow Robert's words), a person learns to fail, correct, learn, apply what was learned, and fail again. This, for Donald J. Trump and Robert T. Kiyosaki, is the path to developing your "Midas Touch." In your failings, there are a few things you have to be aware of, some of which include:

- Inside every mistake is a gem of wisdom.
- Blame means to "be lame."
- Face your mistakes and admit to them.

One of the world's greatest geniuses, Dr. R. Buckminster Fuller, believes that "mistakes are only sins when not admitted." Take 100% responsibility for your mistakes, and in doing that, you find wisdom and gems that give you the energy to move forward. Many people carry around their mistakes, and either they regret having made them or they pretend they never make mistakes and then go on to repeat them. Others become criminals and lie about their mistakes.

The fact remains that if a person makes a mistake and lies, blames, justifies, or pretends they didn't make a mistake, they don't advance. Robert T. Kiyosaki gives an example of former US President Bill Clinton when he lied to the world about having sex with a White House intern. In Robert's view, Clinton could have been one of the greatest presidents but instead he will be remembered for his lack of moral character, for cheating on his wife, and also for lying about it on television. Thus, it takes courage to face your mistakes and admit to them instead of lying about them.

Can you remember how you learned how to ride a bicycle? Can you recall your failures? Did you in any way injure yourself in the process of learning to ride a bicycle? I still have a scar I got while learning. You failed the first, second, third, fourth, and fifth day (even more than that), but later on, you succeeded in riding your bicycle. This applies to life – fail today and succeed tomorrow. The only problem with some people is that when they fail today, they don't dare to rise again. S. Deveraj writes, "Dare to fail, you will excel!" If you're not satisfied with that, recall how many times Jesus Christ failed (and got up) on his way to Calvary. I strongly encourage you to remember to "Dare to fail; you'll excel!"

Never Walk Alone

Jesus Christ knew the importance of togetherness, and that was why he sent out the twelve in pairs. The scripture says, "he made a tour round the village, teaching. Then he summoned the twelve and began to send them out in pairs, giving them authority over the unclean spirits" (Mk. 6:7; Lk. 10:1). Have you ever given a thought to why Jesus had twelve apostles (or disciples, as the case may be)? Why didn't he call only one, two, three, or six people, but instead call twelve energetic, dedicated, and sagacious men? Does this mean he couldn't carry out the work of salvation all alone? I am not sure if that was the reason. Even if he couldn't in his humanity, he could in his divinity. But, in my opinion, the reason was to tell us of the quintessential need for each other – I'm because you're. The message is that for you to accomplish your goals, most of the time you need each other's contribution; you need the association, the allied force, and the co-operation of one another. Ethel Barrymore succinctly opines that "the best time to make friends is before you need them."

Donald J. Trump and Robert T. Kiyosaki in *Midas Touch* reported Lee Iacocca to have said that "in the end, all business operations can be reduced to three words: people, product, and profits. Unless you have got a good team, you can't do much with the other two." The essence of that is the need to work as a TEAM.

In the game of English football (and many other sports), the players might not win if they don't work as a team. In the ecclesiastical sphere, pastors might not be able to carry out their pastoral ministry harmoni-ously if there's no rapport or spirit of brotherhood existing among them. I am a FIFA grade three referee (I was graded in 2013 in Nigeria). Being a member of a referee football association, if there's no co-operation and coordination between the referees (center referee, two linesmen, and the fourth official), it would be difficult (if not impossible) to have fair play in the game. Hence the Liverpool logo is "never walk alone."

In the game of football, the word **TEAM** has been described to stand for:

T for *Together*

E for *Each*

A for *Achieve*

M for *More*

The concept of TEAM goes back to Aristotle's idea of "the whole is greater than the sum of its parts." Cooperation, in the view of Napoleon

Hill, is the beginning of all organized effort. Carnegie accumulated a gigantic fortune through the cooperative efforts of a small group of men numbering not more than a score. The cooperation I emphasize here is of two forms:

1. Cooperation between people who group themselves together or form alliances to attain a given end, under the principle coined by Napoleon Hill known as the "Law of the Mastermind."

2. Cooperation between the conscious and the subconscious minds, which forms a reasonable hypothesis of a person's ability to contact, communicate with, and draw upon infinite intelligence (the Unmoved Mover for Aristotle).

To better explain this principle of "Never Walk Alone," I consider it ad rem to briefly review the physical construction of the human body. I am not an expert in human physiology, so I can only give a researched explanation of how the system communicates. We know that the whole body is traversed by a network of nerves that serve as the channels of communication between the indwelling spiritual ego, which is called the mind, and the functions of the external organism.

I believe that everything in life is relationships. Your ability to form the right relationship with the right people at every stage of your life and career will be the critical determinant of your success and achievement and will have an inordinate impact on how quickly you achieve your goals. The more people you connect with and who recognize you positively, the greater your chances of success in any endeavor; the character of the people with whom you come in contact every day, molded by your surroundings, largely colors your outlook, your estimate of yourself, and your value. Here is my simple formula for success:

Who You Know + What You Know = Success.

To accomplish goals of any kind, you will need the help of several people. The question is who? For Brian Tracy, there are three general categories of people whose help and co-operation you will require, which include:

1. The people in and around your business.

2. Your family and friends.

3. People in groups and organizations outside your business/
   social circle.

Keep the right company (associate with the right people); keep friends or people who are going in the same direction (for birds of a feather always flock together) rather than for company's sake. There are different kinds of people in the world, and it would be wrong for you to think everybody is on the path with you or responding to life in the same way.

From my experience (and my research on Felix McDon), the kinds of people to avoid include:

- Proud and arrogant people.
- The plain, unassuming, and unintelligent individual.
- People with a long memory, that is, people who are like a serpent with a memory that retains information without forgetting quickly.
- The unfortunate and unhappy, who go about with their bad luck.

The company you keep determines the value people will place on you. There is a popular maxim: "Tell me who your friends are, and I will tell you who you are." Keep the company of men who act like eagles so you will learn to soar to great heights. I took it to heart when George Kaitolil said that "we need friends to maintain our peace of mind, to boost our self-respect and to fulfill our human aspiration."

Takeaway for Chapter Three

- In your search or quest to achieve your goals, are you blocked by small difficulty? To be an achiever, not a dreamer, you have to be goal-driven.

- As an achiever, being goal-driven, three essential things are required of you, including deciding what you want, training/empowering your will, and avoiding procrastination.

- Remember that nothing good comes easy. To be successful, you have to be toughened by roadblocks, but after that comes happiness. Just don't stop, for winners never quit and quitters never win.

- As you aspire to greatness in your field of endeavors, who are your mentors, inspirers, and influencers? To be successful, you have to stand on the shoulders of giants.

- You are not a failure until you admit that you have failed. It's not failure but temporary defeat. Learn from the process and move ahead.

- Birds of a feather always flock together. In achieving your goals, choose the right company; learn from them but never be influenced negatively by them.

CHAPTER FOUR

Knock the "T" Off Can't

*"The heights by great men reached and kept weren't attained
by sudden flight, but they, while their companions slept,
were toiling upward in the night."*

—Henry Wadsworth Longfellow

You've Got to Believe it's Possible

It has been said repeatedly that the number-one step to every achievement in life hinges on belief in oneself. Napoleon Hill said, "Whatever the mind can conceive and believe, it can achieve." The mind of a human being is such a powerful instrument, and it can deliver to you literally everything you want.

In his poem "The Man Who Thinks He Can," Walter D. Wintle fleshes out a great psychological truth about belief. The poem emphasizes the power of mindset and self-belief in achieving success. It suggests that one's thoughts and beliefs shape their reality, and those who believe in themselves and their abilities are more likely to overcome challenges and achieve their goals. The poem encourages readers to maintain a positive attitude, believe in their potential, and strive for success with confidence and determination. A section of the poem says:

> If you think you're beaten, you are;
> If you think you dare not, you don't;
> If you like to win, but you think you can't,
> It's almost certain you won't.

I encourage you to go read the entire poem and commit it to memory and use it as a part of your working equipment so as to knock the "T" off "can't" and develop self-confidence. It is very common to hear people say things like "I can't," "It's impossible," or "It can't be done." It becomes a regular confession the moment someone's focus shifts or they take their eyes off the goal and begin to see obstacles rather than the DCA – Definite Chief Aim (as discussed in the previous chapter).

The concepts of Belief and Faith are very similar, though different. Belief, according to James Allen, is an important word in the teachings of the wise, and it features prominently in all religions. For instance, according to Jesus Christ, a certain kind of belief is necessary for salvation or regeneration, and Buddha definitely taught that "right belief" is the first and most essential step in the Way of Truth, as without right belief there can't be right conduct. But this belief (as laid down by the great teachers of ancient times) isn't a belief in any particular school, philosophy, or religion – it consists of an attitude of mind determining the whole course of one's life. Belief and conduct are therefore inseparable, for one determines the other.

Robert H. Schuller, in *Be an Extraordinary Person in an Ordinary World*, helps to explain my point here. Two shoe salesmen were sent to Africa to inspect the potential international market there, like the two spies who returned to Joshua in the Old Testament after reviewing the Promised Land. The salesmen returned to their shoe company with their report. One salesman had a negative report, saying, "There's no market there; nobody wears shoes in Africa." The positive salesman reported, "On the contrary, it's a fantastic opportunity – no one has bought shoes yet."

This story shows that belief is the basis of all action, and in being so, dominates the heart/mind. Every person acts, thinks, and lives in exact accordance with the belief rooted in his or her innermost being. Belief, from my research, has two distinct kinds:

1. Head belief
2. Heart belief

Head belief:

Also called intellectual belief, it isn't fundamental and causative; rather, it's superficial and consequent, and it has no power in the molding of a person's character. For instance, half a dozen people from any creed share the same theological beliefs and profess the same doctrines, yet their characters are vastly different. For James Allen, a person's theological belief is merely his intellectual opinion or view of the universe (for instance on God, the Bible, etcetera).

Heart belief:

In simple terms, these are beliefs a person loves and clings to and fosters in their heart because they believe in them, and believing in them and loving them, they practice them.

Above all else, James (in the strict sense) thinks that belief is of two forms: belief in good and in evil. From another standpoint, faith (of belief, as the case may be) is the head chemist of the mind because when it's blended with the vibration of thought, the subconscious mind instantly picks up the vibration and translates it into physical/material and spiritual equivalents (as in the case of prayer). Faith is a state of mind that may be induced or created by affirmation of repeated instructions to the subconscious mind, through the principle of autosuggestion (a term that applies to all suggestions and all self-administered stimuli that reach one's mind through the five senses). I quite agree with Napoleon, who explained that faith has several roles to play:

- Faith is the "eternal elixir" that gives life, power, and action to the impulse of thought.

- Faith is the starting point of any accumulation of riches.

- Faith is the basis of all "miracles" and mysteries that can't be analyzed by the rules of science.

- Faith is the only known antidote to failure.

- Faith is the element, the "chemical" which, when mixed with prayer, gives one direct communication with Infinite Intelligence (perhaps God).

- Faith is the element that transforms the ordinary vibration of thought, created by the finite mind of humans, into the spiritual equivalent.

- Faith is the only agency through which the cosmic force of infinite intelligence can be harnessed and used.

Scientists believe that humans respond to information flowing into the brain from the outside world. But, nowadays, the reverse is the case. As Napoleon said, "You can be anything you want to be, if only you believe with sufficient conviction and act in accordance with your faith; for whatever the mind can conceive and believe, the mind can achieve."

I love the lyrics of Don Williams's song "I Believe in You." In the song, Don is saying that he doesn't believe in superstars, but only in God and in you. What this means is that you have got to believe in yourself, and also in God, and go for what you believe in because those who win are those who think they can. Let this be one of your daily affirmations: "No matter how bad it is, and how bad it goes, I'm going to make it!" In doing so, don't feel embarrassed, wimpy, and wishy-washy. Just do it!

The books of the scripture have been described by many as the books of belief. Even Jesus Christ demonstrates that by saying, "If you have faith you will say to this mountain be lifted up" (Matt. 21:20). The Law of Belief states that whatever you believe with conviction becomes your reality. For instance, in Matthew 9:29, Jesus Christ says, "According to your faith, it will be done unto you." This invariably implies that your belief becomes your reality.

All improvement in your life comes from changing your beliefs about yourself and your possibilities. Personal growth comes from changing your beliefs about what you can do and about what is possible for you; your self-concept precedes and predicts your levels of performance and effectiveness in everything you do. In other words, it is the master program of the operating system of your mental computer.

Let's review the stories of Albert Einstein, Dr. Albert Schweitzer, Thomas Edison, and other great people:

- Albert Einstein was sent home from school as a young man with a learning disability. His parents were told that he was incapable of being educated. They refused to accept this diagnosis and eventually arranged for him to get an excellent education.

- Dr. Albert Schweitzer had the same problem at school as a boy. His parents were encouraged to apprentice him to a shoemaker so that he would have a safe, secure job when he grew up.

- Thomas Edison was expelled from school in the sixth grade. His parents were told that it would be a waste of time to spend any money educating him because he wasn't particularly smart or capable of being taught anything. Edison went on to become the greatest inventor of the modern age.

The secret is that you are better than you think you are; for God doesn't make any junk.

As Max Lucado (speaker and author) said, "You weren't an accident; you weren't mass produced; you aren't an assembly line product. You were deliberately planned, specially gifted, and lovingly positioned on the earth by the Mastercraftsman." Thus, if you're going to be successful in creating the life of your dreams, you have to believe that you're capable of making it happen. You have to believe in yourself.

This belief in yourself is created by the attitude you develop over time. The choice of what to believe is up to you, for it's not what life hands you but how you respond to it, mentally and physically, that matters most. Don't waste your whole life believing you can't (can't play the piano, can't study, can't lose weight, etcetera), for the words "I can't" disempower you; they actually make you weaker when you say them. What others think about you is none of your business. Join Henry Ford in saying, "I'm looking for a lot of men who have an infinite capacity to not know what can't be done."

As you work to rid of "I can't" from your mental vocabulary, practice this self-confidence formula:

- I know that I can achieve the objective of my DCA. Therefore, I demand of myself persistent, continuous action toward its attainment, and here and now I promise to take such action.

- I realize the dominating thoughts of my mind will eventually reproduce themselves in outward, physical reality. Therefore, I will concentrate for thirty minutes daily upon the task of thinking of the person I intend to become, thereby creating in my mind a clear mental picture of that person.

- I know through the principle of auto-suggestion that any desire I persistently hold in my mind will eventually seek expression through some practical means of attaining the objective. Therefore, I will devote ten minutes daily to demanding of myself the development of self-confidence.

- I have clearly written down a description of my DCA in life. I will never stop trying until I have developed sufficient self-confidence for its attainment.

To look upon this formula is to still be under the shackles of "I can't," but to adhere and practice to get rid of them. Believe in you and you alone, and knock "T" off "I can't."

Acquire Knowledge; Quitters Never Win

Another reformative way of saying the above is: "it's too early to quit, yet too late to stop." Here, I am neither interested in the sophistic Platonic nor in Aristotelian knowledge. Rather, the main concern is knowledge as it is applied. Can you recall the wisdom of these biblical figures?

- Abraham in the book of Genesis 12:10-20 and Genesis 20:1-18.
- Isaac in Genesis 26:7
- Rahab in Joshua 2:1-21
- Jael in Judges 4:17-22
- Tamar in Genesis 38:12-26

- Abigail in 1 Samuel 25:2-42
- Solomon in 1 Kings 3:4-28

The essence of these scriptural references is to expose you to how wisdom or knowledge can assist you to knock the "T" off can't and debunk the idea of quitting. There are different views as to what distinguishes a rich person from a pauper. The number one difference between a rich person and a wretched one is knowledge. In the view of McDon, people are poor because they lack knowledge, and people are rich because they have knowledge. I believe that could be the reason the scripture says that "my people perish for lack of knowledge" (Ho. 4:6). Anyone who lacks knowledge will never see farther beyond his nose, thus remaining at the lowest rung of the ladder.

It was Francis Bacon who once said that "knowledge is power." Knowledge links human intelligence to the realm of possibilities, thereby opening your eyes to the realities of life and placing you above the ordinary. Those who have been able to rise to a position of power, authority, fame, and wealth are those who know.

To many, the word knowledge has a variety of meanings, including education. But the word "education" is a derivation of the Latin word *educo*, meaning "to educe, to draw out or develop from within." An educated person isn't necessarily one who has an abundance of general or specialized knowledge. Educated people have developed the faculties of their minds so that they may acquire anything they want or its equivalent without violating the rights of others.

Napoleon Hill says knowledge has two kinds: general and specialized. General knowledge, no matter how great in quantity or variety it may be, is of little use in the accumulation of money. However, there are seven different types of intelligence. Gardener believes that people have different kinds of intelligence with different ways to learn and process information. We know people who are gifted musicians or athletes. We know people who are math wizards or amazing designers. Here is a concise overview of the various forms of intelligence:

- *Verbal-Linguistic*: People who do well in school, the "A" students, are often of verbal-linguistic intelligence. They are excellent readers and writers. They can quote famous writers and do well on exams. Students who do well linguistically may become lawyers.

- **Logical-Mathematical**: These people love numbers and solving mathematical problems. They can give you the decimal equivalent of fractions faster than you can calculate it on your cell phone or calculator. They're usually "A" students, and many of them go on to attain advanced degrees. Many remain in academia and become teachers, professors, and researchers. Most of them lean toward accounting, computer programming, or engineering.

- **Body-Kinesthetic**: Most athletes are gifted with this intelligence. The most gifted and elite few may go on to become professional athletes or dancers. Some may even lean toward the health or recreation business.

- **Spatial**: Those with this intelligence tend to favor the arts, go on to art school, and some become very successful artists. These people often become architects, interior designers, graphic artists, and website developers.

- **Musical**: Students with this kind of intelligence often dream of being a rock star or lead singer in a band. These people pick up instruments and gain familiarity quickly. They can hear music and almost magically know the notes they're hearing. People with this kind of intelligence are most happy when they're performing and will seek out careers in the musical performing arts.

- **Interpersonal**: This intelligence is important for professional communicators such as politicians, preachers, sales, and advertising specialists.

- **Intrapersonal**: While interpersonal intelligence is your ability to communicate with others, intrapersonal intelligence is your ability to communicate with yourself. People who have this kind of intelligence have control of their own thoughts. Intrapersonal intelligence, also called success intelligence, is required for success with all other intelligence.

Because of the foundational nature of intelligence, Napoleon Hill believes that "the ladder of success is never crowded at the top." It is not crowded because the majority lack the strength, skill, and most importantly, the knowledge or shrewdness to make their marks. The only difference between those who are successful and those who are not is that successful people keep going anyway, despite their difficulties. People doubt their beliefs but believe their doubts. Believe in yourself, and the world will believe in you.

If you have ever considered quitting, read the story behind the writing of *The Power of Positive Thinking* by Norman Vincent Peale. It highlights the importance of perseverance, faith, and the power of positive thinking in overcoming challenges and achieving success. Despite the author's initial setbacks and self-doubt, he learned to embrace his talents and believe in himself. Through determination and support (especially from his wife), he transformed failure into success, thereby demonstrating that with the right mindset and unwavering faith, individuals can overcome obstacles and fulfil their potential.

I dare you to live by faith. Faith goes beyond believing something regardless of the evidence; it is daring to do something regardless of the consequence.

Hang on to the Rule of Five

In computers, we talk about encryption (the processing of a message in order to render it unintelligible to anyone other than the authorized recipients) and decryption (the processing of an encrypted message by an authorized recipient in order to recover the original message). In the previous sections of this book, I have discussed some of the success formulas used by some successful people. Now, how do you achieve your DCA (Definite Chief Aim) from a different standpoint?

In the first account of Creation, God didn't indulge in creation all in a day. Have you pondered why it took God the Creator six days to work and then He rested on the seventh day? The biblical account records, "Let there be light, and there was light. God saw that light was good, and God divided the light from darkness. Evening came, and morning came: the first day?

(Gen.1:1-31). In the New Testament, when Jesus Christ was calling his disciples, did He call all of them on the same day? Not at all. Rather, He was calling them day after day.

I vividly recall one of the things I read about the work of Archbishop Fulton J. Sheen (American archbishop and spiritualist) in *The Priest Is Not His Own*. The archbishop believes that the secret of writing a book is that if the person could write at least a line or a sentence every day, in a year he will have written a book. I believe the archbishop's advice could be applied to other human activities and goals. That is how this book you're reading right now was written. It does work, and I strongly suggest that you try it out!

Day by day, everywhere, we are building our world. Many people have been asking, searching, and seeking the secrets to accomplishing great things. The majority have been on a voyage to find the principles of how to achieve tasks such as: how to play the piano and guitar like a pro, how to write a bestselling book, how to play football, volleyball, lawn tennis, etcetera. The good news is that the secret lies within you.

Small efforts, repeated day in and day out, produce success. Wealth is generated by small efforts that produce big results. Robert G. Allen propounded the 80/20 Rule, which states that 80 percent of our results are as a result of 20 percent of our efforts. This is a little secret that makes a lot of difference.

Jack (together with Hansen), in telling their story of how they made the *New York Times* bestseller list, sought the advice of Ron Scolastico, who told them that no matter how large a tree was, it would have to come down if they took persistent swings at it with a very sharp axe. How very simple and very true, both in writing this book and achieving my other goals. Without a doubt, that is true to the farmer, because it is a daily practice. Think about how a farmer goes about his occupation and the processes involved in his daily business. The first day may be the clearing of the bush or the farmland. The second day may be the gathering together of the junk and burning, followed by ploughing, tilling of the soil, and planting till harvesting time. In other words, every day you are building your world.

In simple terms, every day do five specific things that will move your goal toward completion, and surround yourself with successful people.

As Jim Rohn says, "You're the average of the five people you spend the most time with." How would Jack and Hansen have been a *New York Times* bestseller if not for the expertise of Ron Scolastico? Practice the rule of five and live by it.

Pushing Hard on the Hand of the Clock

I agree 100% with Shammi Sukh, who says that "those who make the worst use of time are the people who complain the most." How an individual uses their time to a great extent contributes to the results they get. Those who waste or misuse their time are more likely to engage in complaining behavior.

For those who believe in God, to what extent do you think God is a just God? I believe God is a fair and just God; He is an impartial God. He gives each person what we individually deserve and need. One of the philosophical mantras of Aristotle was that justice is treating equals equally; and unequals unequally. Now, this doesn't apply to God. God is a just God simply because He gives both the rich and the poor twenty-four hours every day. There's no plus, no minus. He allocates to us (whether working or sleeping) twenty-four hours every single day.

In the view of Brian Tracy, to achieve all your goals and become everything you're capable of becoming, you must put your time under control. This is possible when you practice excellent time-management skills. Sukh believes that managing time isn't about always being busy; it is all about making one's life easy. People who manage their time are the people who make the most of their life.

However, since time management is a skill, I believe it can be learned. No matter how disorganized you have been in the past or how much you have tended to procrastinate or get caught up in low-value activities, you can change. The starting point of time management is for you to determine your goals, and then organize them by priority and value. You need to be absolutely clear, at any given moment, about what's most important to you at that time. To assist you in managing your time well as you aspire to your goals, here are some tips:

1. **Determine your long-term goals**: As philosophy is the handmaid of theology, so clarity is the root of time management. Take the time to sit down with a piece of paper (or it could be sticky notes) and think through what exactly you want to accomplish in each area of your life. Once you're clear about your target (your DCA), come back to the present and plan every minute and hour of every day so you accomplish the most you possibly can with the time allocated to you.

2. **Begin with a list**: The basic tool of time management is a list, organized based on priority. The fact is that you cannot manage time, but you can manage yourself. Because time management requires self-mastery and control, it is a prerequisite that you should plan your life with lists of long-term, medium-term, and short-term goals. Plan every month in advance with a list of the things you want to accomplish during that month. Go by propriety.

3. **Use advance planning**: Don't waste even a minute – begin to plan every week in advance (preferably the Sunday before the week begins). Plan every day in advance (preferably the night before). The good thing is that when you do this, your subconscious mind works on it all night long. When you wake up in the morning, you often have ideas and insights and sometimes hunches to help you accomplish the items on your list. Through advance planning, you're in synchronization with the Law of Attraction – attracting into your life the people, opportunities, and resources that you need to achieve your goals and complete your tasks the very best way.

4. **Separate the urgent from the important**: In the process of managing your time, you must separate urgent tasks from the important ones. Urgent tasks are determined by external pressures and requirements, which require immediate attention. On the other hand, important tasks are those that can contribute to your long-term goal. Some tasks are urgent but not important. The difference is that they produce no results. The final category (which you should avoid completely) is tasks that are neither urgent nor important, like reading the paper at work or going for a long lunch.

5. **Apply the 80/20 rule**: After preliminary planning, apply the 80/20 rule. This rule says that 20 percent of your activities will account for 80 percent of the value of all your activities.

6. **Practice creative procrastination**: Since you cannot do everything, you will have to procrastinate on something. You may ask: which task am I to procrastinate on? My answer is, procrastinate on the tasks that contribute very little to your desired goals and results.

7. **Practice the ABCDE method**: This is another method by which you can set priorities. It requires that you review your list of tasks before you begin and put an A, B, C, D, or E next to each one. The "A" task is something that's very important. A "B" task is something that you should do. A "C" task is a task that would be nice to do but will have no consequence at all. A "D" task is something that you can delegate to someone. An "E" task is something that you can eliminate altogether. Never do a "B" task when there's an "A" task left undone.

8. **The law of the excluded alternative**: This law simply states that doing one thing means not doing something else. Whenever you begin a task of any kind, you're consciously or unconsciously deciding not to do any other task that you could do at that moment. Your ability to choose wisely in terms of what you do first and second, and what you don't do at all, determines your entire life.

9. **Practice concentrating on each task**: Thomas Edison says, "My success is due more to my ability to work continuously on one thing without stopping than to any other single quality." Simply put, once you have selected your "A" task, you start on that task and work on it with single-minded concentration until it's 100 percent complete. You discipline yourself and FOCUS!

10. **Create chunks of time**: Plan your day in advance and create thirty, sixty, and ninety-minute chunks of uninterrupted work time. One great way to create long periods of work time is to rise early and work non-stop, without interruption, on a major task, project, or proposal. You can do this in the evenings or at the weekends. Early Nightingale said, "Every great accomplishment of mankind has been

preceded by an extended period, often over many years, of concentrated effort."

I value my time. It is important that you be mindful of your time; make the most of today by appreciating time. Consider this helpful information:

- To realize the value of "one year," ask a student who failed a grade.
- To realize the value of "one month," ask a teacher who didn't get their month's salary when they depends entirely on their salary as their source of income/financial support.
- To realize the value of "one week," ask the editor of a weekly magazine/newspaper.
- To realize the value of "one hour," ask a factory worker who's paid hourly.
- To realize the value of "one minute," ask a businessperson who missed a flight schedule.
- To realize the value of "one second," ask a person who nearly got involved in an accident.

You can exchange money for an item, and you can exchange an item for money, but you can't exchange money for more time. As you aspire to your goals, beware of time killers. Optimum utilization of time is all about self-management and mind-mastery. Master your time and rule your world!

Takeaway from Chapter Four

► Many people's minds are made up of failure concepts. You've got to believe that things are possible, and you have to play by the rules and principles.

► All great achievements start with self. You are not defeated unless you admit you are.

► Belief in yourself has two distinct methods: head belief and heart belief.

► The majority of people are languishing in all sorts of "evil" (be it financial, spiritual, social, or academic) as a result of lack of knowledge; hence the scripture (Hosea 4:6) says "My people are perishing because they lack knowledge."

► It is too early to quit, for winners never quit and quitters never win.

► There are different types of intelligence and genius; be proud of who you are and hone your own expertise and intelligence.

► Greatness begins in the great magic formula of the sage. Develop your own success formula. If you don't have it, surround yourself and be influenced by those who have it. Remember the story of Jack and Hansen, and Ron Scolastico, and the five rules?

► Time, they say, flies. The earlier you start, the better for you. However, as you make your bed, you lie on it. Control your time and rule your world!

PART TWO
JUST PLAN

CHAPTER FIVE

Stop Thinking, Start Planning

"Read not to contradict and confute, nor to believe and take for granted, nor to find fault and discourse, but to weigh and consider."

—Francis Bacon

Zero-Based Thinking: The Strength of Character

Earl Nightingale once said that "your problem is to bridge the gap between where you are now and the goals you intend to reach." Imagine that you were going to take a long trip across the country – what would be your first step? I guess the first step would be to choose your destination and then get a road map to determine the very best way to get there. Each day before you start out, you would use a map leading to the exact place you intend to head. However, once you have your DCA, the next step is for you to analyze your starting point, to plan your voyage. This is in line with what Jack Welch called the "Reality Principle" of getting from where you're to where you want to be. For Welch, the Reality Principle is the ability to see the world as it really is, not as you wish it were.

From another perspective, assuming you have decided to lose weight, the very first step you would take is to weigh yourself, and from there you will measure your progress. If you decide to begin an exercise program, the first step would be to determine how much you are to exercise each day. If you want to earn more money, the first step is to sit down and determine exactly how much you're earning right now and how much you intend to earn in the future. The tighter and more accurate your calculations (precisely, your planning) regarding what you intend to have, the better and faster you can improve in that area.

As you aspire and project your Definite Chief Aim, have you taken the time to ask: "Is my goal realistic, based on where I am today and the time I have allocated to get where I intend to go?" If the answer is NO, I would advise you to honestly and completely revise your calculations and projections.

Regarding zero-based thinking, experts like Brian Tracy have some great exercises:

- Knowing what I know now, is there anything that I'm doing today (even now) that I wouldn't start again if I want to do it over?
- How can I stop holding myself back with past faulty decisions?

Circumstances change, and given that, be prepared to make necessary changes (remember to change your "R" in "E" to get your desired "O"). Life is like a grindstone. Whether it grinds you down or pushes you up depends on what you're made of.

In giving an account of what strength of character is, Robert T. Kiyosaki says how he was able to sell two million copies of *Rich Dad Poor Dad* after his television show with Oprah Winfrey. After appearing on the show, he made $5 million in one hour. In his view, the strength of character lies in the stability to handle the daily challenges, the ups and downs and wins and losses, as you intend to swim with the sharks without being eaten alive.

There are smart, well-educated, talented people everywhere who fail to develop their God-given talents or gifts. We have seen people whose lives are tales of woes, tragedy, or betrayal, who blame their failures or a bad start in life on other people. You may also know people who have a great idea about how to make millions of dollars but are too lazy to get off the couch. Above all, you may know people who live in the future and fail to act today (thereby debunking zero-based thinking). In all these, it is with the strength of character, that inner urge to still move ahead, that you can attain your goal.

Sacrifice is a price to pay for the acquisition of strength of character. Success requires sacrifice. The greatest sacrifice made by any known person on earth was by Jesus Christ, which is seen in His death on the cross for the salvation of the human race and His resurrection. It is through this sacrifice that He rose to His glory. In other words: no cross, no crown. Clean up your messes (what Dale Carnegie called Stupid Things Done), your mistakes and stupidity.

As a way of zero-basing your thinking and developing strength of character, there are two preliminary and important skills you need to have, which include:

- The cultivation of concentration.
- The practice of meditation

The cultivation of concentration:

Jesus Christ, after any of his public appearances, would go up a mountain to a quiet place and have a private moment. The Bible says, "After he had come down from the mountain" (Matt. 8:1), "After sending the crowds away he went up into the hills by himself to pray" (Matt. 14:22-23), "And leaving them standing there, he went away" (Matt. 16:4), "Six days later, Jesus took with him Peter and James and his brother John and led them up a high mountain where they could be alone" (Matt.17:1). Not only Jesus Christ, but some others like Moses (Ex. 32:1; 33:18-19) and Elijah did as well (1 kgs.19:1-14).

Concentration, according to James Allen, or the bringing of the mind to a center and keeping it there, is vitally necessary to the accomplishment of any task. It is the father of thoroughness (which consists in doing little things as though they were the greatest things in the world) and the mother of excellence. As a faculty, it is not an end in itself but is an aid to all faculties, all work. Every successful person, in whatever direction of their success, practices concentration. Every time someone becomes absorbed in a book or task or is rapt in devotion or assiduous in duty, concentration is brought into play.

Concentration is an aid to the doing of something; it is not the doing of something in itself. By analogy, a ladder has no value in and of itself, only insofar as it enables a person to reach for something they wouldn't or couldn't otherwise reach. In like manner, concentration is that which enables the mind to accomplish with ease what would be otherwise impossible to accomplish.

But then, what could be the likely enemy of concentration? James Allen thinks the great enemy of concentration (probably of all skill and power) is a wavering, wandering, undisciplined mind, and it's in overcoming this that concentration is acquired.

It is governed by the underlying principle of all development, namely practice. Continuous practice makes you better. To be able to paint, one must know how to use a tool skillfully. To become learned, you must learn; to become wise, you must do wise things; and to successfully concentrate your mind, you must concentrate on it. One of my school mentors when I was learning to play the piano once told me that to play the piano, I must get involved and start to play.

The beginning of concentration is to go to your daily task and put your mind on it, bringing all your intelligence and mental energy to focus upon what has to be done, and every time the thoughts are found wandering aimlessly away, they should be brought promptly back to the thing at hand. This focusing of one's thought and energy and will upon the doing of things may be difficult at first (as everything worth acquiring is difficult) but through daily efforts, strenuously made and patiently followed up, it can be achieved. Achieving it brings about a measure of self-control (you could also call it mind control), which will help you have a mind that is strong and penetrating and able to bear upon any work undertaken; a mind that will quickly comprehend all the details of the work and dispose of them with accuracy and dispatch.

Through long years of experiment and researching the works of experts, I have realized there are four stages of concentration, which include:

- Attention
- Contemplation
- Abstraction
- Activity in repose

At first, the thoughts are arrested, and the mind is fixed upon the object of concentration, which is the task at hand. This is called attention. The mind is then roused into vigorous thought about the way of proceeding with the task, which is called contemplation. Protracted contemplation leads to a condition of mind in which the doors of the senses are all closed against the entrance of outside distraction, the thoughts wrapped in and solely and intensely centered upon the work at hand. This is called abstraction. The mind thus centered in profound cognition reaches a state in which the maximum work is accomplished with the minimum friction; this is the activity of repose. Each stage of concentration has its particular power. The first stage, when perfected, leads to usefulness; the second stage leads to skill, ability, and talent; the third leads to originality and genius, while the fourth leads to mastery and power, which makes leaders and teachers of men.

The practice of meditation:

When aspiration is united with concentration, the result is meditation. When a person intensely desires to reach and realize a higher, purer, and more radiant life than the merely worldly and pleasure-loving life, he engages in aspiration; and when he earnestly concentrates his thoughts upon the finding of that life, he practices meditation, says James Allen. Concentration is necessary for worldly success; meditation is necessary for spiritual success. Worldly skills and knowledge are acquired by concentration, while spiritual skills and knowledge are acquired by meditation. By concentration, a person may acquire the wonderful comprehension and vast power of a Caesar; by meditation, he may reach the divine wisdom and perfect peace of Buddha.

The perfection of concentration is power, while the perfection of meditation is wisdom. By concentration, people acquire skill in the doing of things of life (in science, trade, etcetera), but by meditation, they acquire skill in life itself (in right living, enlightenment, wisdom). Meditation is more difficult to practice than concentration because it involves more self-discipline than concentration. For Allen, the principle of meditation is two-fold, namely:

- Purification of the heart by repetitive thought on pure things
- Attainment of divine knowledge by embodying such purity in practice.

In the practice of meditation, one shouldn't confuse it with reverie. To differentiate, reverie is a loose dreaming into which a person falls, while meditation is purposeful thinking into which they rise. Reverie is easy and pleasurable; meditation is at first difficult and irksome. For a detailed distinction between reverie and meditation, I have created the table below.

Reverie	Meditation
A desire to avoid exertion.	Increase of both physical and mental energy.
A desire to experience the pleasure of dreaming.	A strenuous striving after wisdom.
An increasing distaste for one's worldly duties.	A decrease of irksomeness in the performance of duty.
A desire to shirk one's worldly responsibilities.	A fixed determination to faithfully fulfill all worldly responsibilities.
Fear of consequences.	Freedom from fear.
A wish to get money with less effort.	Indifference to riches.
Lack of self-control.	Possession of self-control.

That's a lot of information in the table above. There are certain times, places, and conditions in and under which it is impossible or difficult to meditate and others wherein meditation is rendered more accessible.

Times, Places, and Conditions in which Meditation is Impossible:

- At or immediately after meals.
- In places of pleasure such as nightclubs, amusement parks, or busy shopping malls.
- In crowded places.
- While walking rapidly.
- While lying in bed in the morning.

- While smoking.
- While lying on a couch or bed for physical or mental relaxation.

Times, Places, and Conditions in Which Meditation is Difficult:

- At night.
- In a luxuriously furnished room.
- While sitting on a soft, yielding seat.
- When with company.
- When the body is weary.
- If the body is given too much food.

Times, Places, and Conditions in Which it's Best to Meditate:

- Very early in the morning.
- Immediately before meals.
- In solitude.
- In the open air or a plainly furnished room.
- While sitting on a hard seat.
- When the body is strong and vigorous.
- When the body is modestly and plainly clothed.
- Meditation acts as a catalyst that spurs you to your goal. And success, they say, is 99% perspiration and 1% inspiration.

Unlock Your Inborn Creativity; It's Your Birthright

It is a surprise and a shame that many people are untrue to themselves by not recognizing what they have, thereby running from pillar to post. As a result of this lack of self-awareness and confidence, they appear insignificant/diminished in comparison to what they could achieve if they fully embraced their potential. Also, by not claiming what is rightfully theirs, they relinquish control over their own destiny and allow others to determine their fate.

Let me share an enriching narrative about a man from the Orient (the eastern part of the world, especially China and Japan) who travelled around the world in search of the smartest guru. He was told that a wise old man lived in a cave high up in the Himalayas, so that was his final destination. He loaded his horse down with supplies and set off across the mountains and deserts to find this man of wisdom.

After months of traveling, he came to the foot of the Himalayas. He led his horse up a narrow path until he came to a cave. "Are you the guru who's known for his wisdom around the world?" he called out. He waited and waited until finally the old man walked out into the light so that he could be seen. "Old man, how can I become brilliant? Where can I find wisdom?" the weary traveler asked. The wise old guru raised his head and looked into the anxious man's eyes. "Where can you find your horse?" And with that, he turned and walked back into the dark cave.

His horse was with him all the time; brilliance and the capacity for wisdom were with him all the time. So it is right there, deep inside of each and every one of us, but we don't believe it. You have the ability. You have got that gift!

It may be as a result of human ideas, which according to Robert Collier, in *The Secret of the Ages,* "make every thought, every fact that comes into your mind pay you a profit. Make it work and produce for you. Think of things not as they're but as they may be. Don't merely dream but create." Do you recognize the capacity of the human brain and what it is made of?

It was a common thing among students when I was an undergraduate to say that anyone who studied too much was going to experience brain fatigue. With time, I realized that was false. I researched an expert in the field of brain composition who had authored several books on creativity, learning, and intelligence, Tony Buzan, and I found out that the mental potential of the average person is largely untapped and virtually unlimited. Your neocortex, your thinking brain, has approximately one hundred billion cells or neurons. Each of these cells bristles like a porcupine with as many as twenty thousand ganglia or fibers that connect it to other brain cells. These cells are, in turn, connected and interconnected to thousands and millions of other cells (like an electric grid that lights up and powers a large city). Each cell, and each connection, stands as an element of mental energy or information that's available to every other cell. What this points out is that the complexity of your brain is beyond belief or imagination. Also, it means that the number of combinations and permutations of brain connections you have is greater than the number of molecules in the known universe.

Brian Tracy discovered that an average person uses about one or two percent of their brain capacity for a hundred percent of their functioning in life and work. The rest, Tracy calls "reserve capacity." In his view, also, most people go to their graves with their music still in them. According to research conducted by Professor Sergei Yeframov in Russia some years ago, if you could use just 50% of your existing mental capacity, you could complete the doctoral requirements of a dozen universities, learn a dozen languages with ease, and memorize the entire twenty-two volumes of the Encyclopedia Britannica.

That's startling right? Creativity is a natural ability – it is a gift from the creator to his creatures. Can you remember how creative you were when you were still young, between the ages of three and five? Also, can you rate the level of your creativity as you went through school? But what is the result of not tapping into the creativity of your brain? Your creativity or mental acumen is like a muscle; if you don't use it, you lose it. We know that if you don't exercise your muscle and stretch it regularly, it becomes weak and ineffective. So is the nature of human creativity.

The good thing about your mental creativity is that it is never too late for tapping and using it at a higher level. Each time you use more of your existing brainpower, you become more capable of thinking better, with greater clarity. In order to activate the inborn creative power, I recommend you practice mind-storming regularly.

The most important and powerful technique in unlocking and improving your mental creativity and intelligence is "mind-storming." Begin this exercise by first getting a clean sheet of paper. At the top of the page, write your goal or problem in the form of a question. Know that the simpler and more specific the question, the better quality answer you generate in response to it. For example, instead of writing "how can I play a musical instrument?" you write "how can I play the piano in six months?"

Each of your answers should be written using what Brian Tracy called the "Three P Formula –

Personal, Positive, and in the Present tense." The idea behind the formula is to frame affirmations/goals in a way that maximizes their effectiveness. By making statements personal, positive, and in the present tense, individuals can better align their thoughts and beliefs with their desired outcomes, enhancing their motivation and likelihood of success.

Once you have written your question at the top of the page, you then discipline yourself to generate as many answers as possible to that question. Whatever your answers are, put them into action immediately. Tell yourself to do something, do anything.

Based on my experience, the very best time to do this exercise is first thing in the morning. Afterwards, you immediately get busy and implement one of your answers. Imagine that you were to perform this exercise every morning, five days per week – You would generate one hundred ideas per week. If you practice fifty weeks per year, you will generate five thousand ideas over the course of the next twelve months. If you were then to implement one new idea each day to help you move faster toward your goals, this would amount to 250 new ideas per year. Imagine that!

There are thousands of exercises you can engage in that act as a catalyst in order to unlock your inborn creativity. But the one last factor I recommend for you is called the "development of Plan B." Each time I think of Plan B, Otto Von Bismarck (the "Iron Chancellor" of nineteenth century Germany) comes to mind. Bismarck was considered to be the finest statesman of his age. He was famous for a lot of things, including having a backup plan, which became known as a "Bismarck Plan," or "Plan B."

What is Plan B all about? It simply means having as many options as you can in your aspiration to greatness. The more options you have, the greater mental freedom you have as well. The more alternatives you have thought through and developed, the greater power you have in any situation. Use your creativity to develop options and alternatives; if you don't use it, you lose it.

Give Each Person What He Deserves

According to an African proverb "A society without a mad person loses something; but woe to me if it comes from my mother's womb." Two incidents that depict the meaning of this quote came to mind. Let's look at them.

Narrative 1:

Sometime ago, during my third-year undergraduate studies, I was chatting with one of my friends. My friend said something that startled me and that was that people who are not mentally stable have roles to play in society. To substantiate his view, he told me a story of what happened in a small town in the eastern part of Nigeria, where a madman met a woman and said: "Angela, lover of bread, if your son comes back and gives you bread, don't dare eat it."

Coincidentally, it happened that the son came back and gave his mother, Angela, a loaf of bread. The son wanted to use his mother for a money ritual – the practice of sacrificing someone (literarily killing someone) with the intention of attracting wealth, fortune/financial success. But unfortunately for him, it didn't work out. Later on, when the date given to him for the money ritual expired, he became mad.

I ask again, do mad people play any role in society? Through the intervention of the madman (through his message), Angela was saved from being harmed.

Narrative 2:

A nobody today can be somebody tomorrow; do not underrate anybody or take them for granted. As Plato says, appearance is deceptive. You cannot know who people really are by the way they appear to you. Most people have formed a habit to judge people by mere appearance based on the clothes they wear, where they live, their place of work, etcetera. Do not be too sure of anybody; the person you see to be of little importance today may become a person of power tomorrow.

A man whose wife was sick went to the hospital. On reaching the hospital, the man was asked to give them about $2000 before his wife could be admitted to the hospital. Having no money with him, he decided to return home in search of money. On his way, he came across a madman who lived on the street near his house. Based on the look on his face, the madman asked him if there was a problem. He looked at the madman and refused to answer. He went to his friends and neighbors to plead with them for some money.

Coming back to his house, he saw the madman, who asked him again why he looked annoyed. Once again, he ignored the madman, who decided to block the road and not to allow him to pass through until he was willing to disclose the problem. Left with no option, the man opened up and told the madman why he was there. In the end, the madman went to his room and brought out the exact amount the man needed to pay for his wife to be admitted into the hospital and gave it to him. In total amazement, the man was unable to move for over ten minutes. What a surprise!

In your aspiration for success, don't take people for granted. The person you ignore today may occupy a position of honor tomorrow; he may become the person who will sign a certain document that you need to get the job you're looking for, or he may be in a position to offer you the job you're longing for. The person who is at the lowest rung of the ladder today may through little effort, combined with the divine intervention of God, find himself at the top of the ladder of life. Remember, nothing in life is constant and permanent except change. The future is like a pregnant woman filled with uncertainties. Learn to see through appearances and their contradictions. Never trust the version that people give of themselves. It is on this that the scripture admonishes "Don't compliment a person on his good looks. On the other hand, don't look down on someone who is unattractive; compared to most flying things, a bee is very small, but the honey it makes is the sweetest of foods" (Sirach 11:2-6).

Martin Luther King Jr. was the son of a slave, but today he is seen and respected as a hero. America designates a whole day as a public holiday in his honor. Barak Obama became a legend, a world hero, and an inspirer. His name rings bells in the minds of people who are interested in world events. The list could go on and on. Michael Jackson, Haile Selaise of

Ethiopia, Idi Amin of Uganda, Mohammed Ali, Buddha, and Confucius were very popular personalities in their various endeavors and chosen paths. All these people were looked down upon in the past, but today their names are inscribed in the annals of the world as heroes.

Experience the Power of the Mind

"Mind is the master," said James Allen, and "as a man thinketh in his heart, so is he," says the book of Proverbs (Pr. 23:7). These adages apply to every condition and circumstance of human endeavor. Each of us is literally what we think, our character being the complete sum of all our thoughts. As a tree springs from and could not be without the seed, so every one of our acts springs from the hidden seeds of thought and could not have appeared without them. This applies as equally to spontaneous and unpremeditated acts as to those that are deliberately executed.

Jesus Christ, in recognizing the power of the human mind, tells a parable and gives an injunction in the scripture. He says, "The kingdom of heaven is like treasure hidden in a field which someone has found; he hides it again, goes off happy, sells everything he owns and buys the field" (Matt. 13:44-46). Again, the scripture says, "I tell you solemnly, if you have faith and don't doubt at all, not only will you do what I have done to the fig tree, but even if you say to this mountain, get up and throw yourself into the sea, it will be done" (Matt. 21:20-22).

Analogically, the human mind might be likened to a garden, which may be intelligently cultivated or allowed to run wild. But whether cultivated or neglected, it must and will bring forth. If they are not useful seeds, then an abundance of useless weed-seeds will fall, accumulate, and reproduce their own kind. Just as the gardener cultivates the plot, keeping it free from weeds and cultivating the flowers and fruits, so may we tend the garden of our mind, weeding out all the wrong, useless, and impure thoughts and cultivating toward perfection the flowers and fruits of right, useful, and pure thoughts.

Orison Swett Marden once was of the view that, "it's a psychological law that whatever we wish to accomplish we must impress on the subjective or sub-conscious minds." In line with that, John Boyle, added that "whatever you can hold in your mind on a continuing basis, you can have." Whatever you impress deeply into your subconscious mind will eventually be expressed in your external world.

It has been proved, beyond every reasonable doubt, by scientists that the human mind is both a broadcasting and a receiving station. Thomas Paine was one of the great minds of the American Revolutionary Period. He helped in drawing up the Declaration of Independence and persuading those who appended their signature on that document to translate it into terms of reality. In speaking of the source of his great storehouse of knowledge, Paine states that "any person, who has made observations on the state of progress of the human mind, by observing their own, cannot but have observed that there are two distinct classes of thoughts – those that we produce in ourselves by reflection and the act of thinking, and those that bolt into the mind of their own accord."

A human being, in its totality, is a mind with a body. As a result of that, you possess mystical powers (both known and unknown). I tell people that if they should discover the kinds of powers they possess, from that very moment they will begin to fear themselves. Remember what transpired between the serpent and Eve (according to scriptural injunction). The serpent said, "No, you will not die! God knows in fact that on the day you eat it your eyes will be opened, and you will be like gods, knowing good and evil" (Gen. 3:1-7). Clear the cobwebs from your thinking and dare to explore the powers of your mind.

Some of the benefits that awaits you immediately when you discover and explore the God-given powers include:

- Physical, mental, and moral health, happiness, and wealth.
- Success in your chosen field of endeavor
- A means to affect, use, control, or harmonize with powers known and unknown.

Earlier on, we saw that a person is a mind with a body. Let me try to explain that a bit before moving on. The body is the mechanism that controls and through which your mind functions. James Allen, on the effect of thought on health and body, is of the opinion that the body is the servant of the mind; it obeys the operations of the mind, whether they be deliberately chosen or automatically expressed. At the bidding of unlawful thoughts, the body sinks rapidly into disease and decay; at the command of glad and beautiful thoughts, it becomes clothed with youthfulness and beauty. James advised us to be aware that "people will continue to have impure and poisoned blood so long as they propagate unclean thoughts." Out of a clean heart comes a clean body, out of a defiled mind precedes a defiled life and a corrupt body. Change of diet won't help us if we won't change our thoughts. "If you would perfect your body," said James, "guard your mind. If you would renew your body, beautify your mind."

In a simple form, your mind is of two parts (according to statistical analysis):

1. Conscious mind
2. Subconscious mind

They both synchronize, and they work together. In the classical work of Napoleon Hill and W. Clement Stone (*Success Through a Positive Mental Attitude*), they opined that scientists have learned a great deal about the conscious mind, yet it has been less than a hundred years since we began to explore the vast unknown territory of the subconscious mind.

The Conscious mind:

This is the generalissimo in charge of all your mental forces. It can plan ahead and get things done as it plans. Or it can drift along haphazardly, a creature of impulse, at the mercy of events in the current of life. In an attempt to bring it down to its zero point, when you say, "I see, I hear, I smell, I touch," it's your conscious mind that's saying that; thus, it's the force governing the five physical senses.

In the words of Dr. Robert Collier, the author of *The Secret of the Ages*, "It's the phase of mind with which you feel and reason; that's the phase of mind with which everyone is familiar." Above that, it's through your conscious mind that you can reach the subconscious and also the super-conscious mind. Your conscious mind is the porter at the door and the watchman at the gate. It is to the conscious mind that the subconscious looks for its impressions; it depends on the conscious for the teamwork necessary to get successful results. In likening the conscious mind to the subconscious, you wouldn't expect much from an army (no matter how fine its soldiers are) whose generals never planned ahead. Also, you wouldn't look for a good score from a bad team whose pitcher was at odds with the catcher.

The most important province of your conscious mind, as Robert Collier puts it, is to center your thoughts on the thing you want, believe that you will receive it than focusing on the possibility of failure. If you gain the ability to do that, nothing is impossible to you.

The Subconscious mind:

There are certain occurrences that may be a little bit difficult, if not impossible, for us to give their accounts. For instance, can you tell how much water, how much salt, how much of each different element there should be in your blood to maintain its proper specific gravity if you're leading an ordinary sedentary life? Do you know how much water you should drink to neutralize the excess salt in saltfish? How much do you lose through perspiration?

If you don't know, something in you does – the subconscious mind. For Robert Collier, the subconscious mind is one of those "Lightning Calculators." In brief, Dr. Geo. C. Pitier writes that "the subconscious mind is a distinct entity. It occupies the whole human body, and, when not opposed in any way, it has absolute control over all the functions, conditions, and sensations of the body." In *Practical Psychology and Sex Life* by David Bush, Dr. Wilbigler was quoted to have said that "it's the mind that carries on the work of assimilation and up-building while we sleep, it reveals to us things that the conscious mind has no conception of until the consummation has occurred. It can communicate with other minds without the ordinary physical means. It gets glimpses of things that ordinary sight can't behold. It makes God's presence an actual, realizable fact, and keeps the personality in peace and quietness. It warns of approaching danger . . . It heals the body and keeps it in good health, if it's all encouraged."

The subconscious mind is called the subjective mind because it doesn't decide and command. Its nature is to do what it is told or what really, in your heart of hearts, you desire. The geniuses of literature, art, commerce, government, politics, and invention are, according to scientists, ordinary people like you and me who have learned how to draw upon their subconscious mind. For instance, Sir Isaac Newton was reported to have to acquire his marvelous knowledge of mathematics and physics with no conscious effort. Mozart said of his beautiful symphonies that "they just came to him." Descartes, Robert Collier said, had no formal education.

Ella Wheeler Wilcox (a famous poet and journalist of the late 19th and early 20th century), gave evidence of her understanding of the power of the subconscious mind by saying, "You never can tell what a thought will do in bringing you hate or love – for thoughts are things, and their airy wings are swifter than carrier doves." In simple terms, thoughts have a tangible impact on our lives, as they can either attract love or hate, depending on their nature. Also, thoughts have the ability to travel swiftly and influence our emotions and relationships.

Life, as we have it today, has undergone revolutions and transformations. For instance, first came the Stone Age (when life was for the strength of arm or fleet of foot); then there was the Iron Age (the time when the strong lorded it over the weak). Later came the Golden Age (riches took the path of strength), and finally the Information or Atomic Age, which is really the age of mind (when every person can be his own master, where poverty and circumstance no longer hold power, and the lowliest creature in the land can win a place side by side with the highest).

The power to be what you want to be, to get what you desire, to accomplish whatever you're striving for, abides in you. The "kingdom" is within you. Now, for the subconscious mind to work, it needs something – activation. How do I activate this mind? Your subconscious mind is only activated, Brian Tracy believes, by affirmative statements phrased in the present tense. Therefore, write down your goals as though you have already accomplished them. Don't forget to utilize the Three P Formula – Positive, Present, and Personal. Your subconscious mind works like a massive computer that's never turned off to help bring your goals into reality. Almost without you doing anything, your goals will begin to materialize in your life, sometimes in the most remarkable and unexpected ways.

Takeaway from Chapter Five

► Success, they say, leaves clues. Many principles have been laid down for a quick and step-by-step formula to success, one of which is zero-based thinking, which is your strength of character.

► Virtue is knowledge. Since knowledge can be taught, virtue invariably can be learned. To practice zero-based thinking, two things need to be learned and two skills need to be adopted: the cultivation of concentration, and the practice of meditation.

► The four stages of concentration include: attention, contemplation, abstraction, and activity in repose.

► Many people go to their graves with their music still playing in them. Success is your birthright; thus, unlock your inborn creativity with just a little effort.

► The greatest mistake you can make in life, as you strive to achieve greatness, is to take people for granted – don't underestimate anybody. Remember, a nobody today can be somebody tomorrow.

► Mind is the master; you are what you think. The success you seek is right within you, and it just requires a small amount of effort to unlock. Let the real you please stand up!

CHAPTER SIX

To Live in the Present Day

"You have to know what you stand for,
not just what you stand against."

—Margaret Atwood, author

Boost your Self-Esteem!

Honestly, I am not an expert when it comes to human psychology. My explanations here come from my experience and research. There are things that you may need to acquire and develop in your desire to ascend the ladder of success, one of which is self-esteem. According to the New Webster's Dictionary of the English Language, and Oxford Advanced Learner's Dictionary 6th edition, self-esteem is one's good opinion of one's dignity or worth, or a feeling of being happy with one's character and abilities. In short, it is to think highly of yourself.

There are so many fantastic books that address issues concerning self-esteem. Having low self-esteem is a bit like having malaria or cancer. It's there within us and pops up to the surface now and then in an utterly disconcerting way. Summarizing Sue Atkinson (author of *Building Self-Esteem*), low self-esteem exerts greater strains than something like malaria because:

- It influences the whole of our life, with unremitting devastation on our day-to-day actions.
- It affects our thoughts and beliefs about the world.
- It affects all our relationships.

- It can mean that we achieve far less than our potential in the main aspects of our lives.
- It lowers the quality of our life.

Whence then comes this evil threat to humanity? Self-esteem comes not from a germ but from our beliefs about ourselves that we developed as we grew up and from the other struggles of life. Presumably, it has its roots in:

- The ways that our families treated us early on.
- The culture of the society in which we live.
- Our responses to our wider families, friends, and even enemies.
- Our natural aptitudes that we were born with or without and our unique personality.

On the other hand, low self-esteem (as I have observed and from research) stems from:

- Being told we are unwanted or feeling unwanted.
- Some kind of abuse, either physical, emotional, verbal, or sexual.
- Being teased (a version of verbal abuse).
- Being bullied at school or at home.
- Having our failures, shortcomings, or difficulties emphasized.
- Being manipulated by someone powerful.
- Having busy parents and lacking attention from them, maybe with another child in the family being the favorite.
- Receiving heavy criticism.
- Feeling abandoned or rejected due to death, a marriage breakdown, being split from a brother or sister, or being taken away from one situation and put into another.

The good news is that low self-esteem can be boosted or built-up. John Peers believes that "you can't lead a cavalry charge if you think you look funny on a horse." People with low self-esteem rarely achieve their potential; they won't take risks, they wallow in self-blame, they cannot trust others, and they remain in the background when they are needed up front.

The most noteworthy breakthrough in psychology and human performance in the twentieth century was the discovery of the "self-concept." Your self-concept is the bundle of beliefs that you have about yourself. It is the way you see yourself and think about yourself in every area of your life. Your self-concept is the "master program" of your subconscious computer. It is like an operating system that determines everything you say, think, feel, and do.

In his book *The Psychology of Selling*, Brian Tracy describes self-concept as that inner urge that propels a seller to improve in his sale. For example, if you have a high, positive self-concept with regard to yourself, then prospecting or networking is not a problem for you. You get up in the morning eager to call on new people. You are competent and confident in the area of lead generation, so your sales pipeline is always full. If you have a poor self-concept with regard to prospecting, you will approach it with fear and anxiety. You will avoid it wherever possible. The very idea of prospecting will make you tense and uneasy. You will do as little of it as possible and continually look for ways to avoid it.

Self-esteem could also mean self-image; a person's mental picture of themselves – who they are, how they look, what they are good at, and even their weaknesses, which are often determined by:

- One's personal convictions.
- The impression people give about them.
- Their life experience.

Self-image can be very positive (based on confidence in personal thought and actions), or negative (when it makes someone doubtful of his or her capabilities and ideas). If you have a negative self-image, it limits your capability of what you can achieve. Thus, to enhance your chance of success, you should create a positive image of yourself with such affirmation as "I can" rather than "I cannot." Oftentimes, the cause of poor self-image may be the result of accumulated criticisms a person received as a child that have led to a damaging view of themselves. What we believe about ourselves to be true comes true. If you lack self-confidence, it will show by the way you carry yourself around; your body language and posture definitely portray what is inside you.

Perusing through a book by Nigerian author Barnabas, I realized that "we act as we feel," and also, "if we feel courageous, we act boldly; and if we act boldly, we feel courageous, because action and feelings cannot be independent of each other." To Dorothy Briggs, our self-image influences the kind of friends we choose, how well we get along with people, and the kind of person that we marry. For Joyce Brothers, "our self-image has direct influence on the clothes we wear, the profession we choose, the mate we select, the habit we acquire and our moral conduct."

Now, the good thing about low self-esteem is that it can be enhanced, upgraded, and boosted by consciously taking these steps:

- Be optimistic and turn every adversity into an opportunity for good.
- Start to "Act As If," knowing what you want out of life and working toward becoming the kind of person you want to be.
- Discuss your feelings with those who understand you.
- Mind the kind of words you use.
- Avoid negative/self-depressive thoughts.
- Don't underrate yourself.
- Aim at accomplishing rather than perfection.
- Practice! Practice! Practice!

Be optimistic, because optimism sees success where others see failure, and sunshine where others see shadows and storms. A story titled "The Window," told by Jack Canfield in *Chicken Soup for the Soul*, goes like this: Two men who were ill occupied the same hospital room. One was allowed to sit up in his bed for an hour each afternoon to help drain the fluid from his lungs. His bed was next to the room's only window. The other spent all his time flat on his back. The men talked for hours on end. They spoke of their wives and families, their homes, their jobs, their involvement in the military service, the places they had been to on vacation.

Every afternoon when the man in the bed by the window could sit up, he would pass the time by describing to his roommate all the things he could see outside the window. The man in the other bed began to live for those one-hour periods when his world would be broadened and enlivened by all the activity and color of the world outside. The window overlooked a park with a lovely lake. Ducks and swans played on the water while the children sailed their boats. Young lovers walked arm amidst flowers of every color and a fine view of the city skyline could be seen in the distance. As the man by the window described all this in exquisite detail, the man at the other side of the room would close his eyes and imagine the picturesque scene.

One warm afternoon, the man by the window described a parade passing by. Although the other man couldn't hear the band, he could see it in his mind's eye as the gentleman by the window portrayed it with descriptive words.

Weeks passed and one morning, the day nurse arrived bringing water for their baths, only to find the lifeless body of the man by the window. He had died peacefully in his sleep. She was saddened and called the hospital attendants to take the body away. As soon as it seemed appropriate, the other man asked if he could be moved next to the window. The nurse was happy to make the switch, and after making sure he was comfortable, she left him alone. Slowly, painfully, he propped himself up on one elbow to take his first look at the real world outside. He strained to turn slowly and looked out of the window beside the bed. It faced a blank wall. The man asked the nurse what could have compelled his deceased roommate to describe such a wonderful thing outside this window. The nurse responded that the man was blind and couldn't see the wall. She said, "Perhaps he just wanted to encourage you."

What a story! To get rid of your low self-image, elevate other people. Teach them something to improve their lives. Serve them, and in Zig Ziglar's words, remember that "to achieve success, help others achieve theirs first, before yours."

Why Be Poor? Increase Your Financial IQ

In an attempt to bring people to consciousness, Melvin Powers once remarked that, "the uncommon man is merely the common man thinking and dreaming of success and in more fruitful areas." Have you ever spent time pondering why the three servants at the parable of the talents were not given the same amount of money? Why is it that their master did not allot to them the same amount of money? God saw the need of man to widen his monetary genius and become an expert on issues dealing with money (Matt. 25:14-30). Like the army recruiting poster, one of your goals is to "be all you can be" by becoming an expert in money language.

One quality of the most successful people is that at a certain point in their careers they decide to commit to excellence, thereby studying the language and playing by the rules of money. Do not get frightened at the mention of money; remember, no one is better than you, and every person is smart in different areas. People who are doing well in money marketing learned the essential skills. If you have not gotten it yet, it simply means you are in the process of doing that.

Everything worthwhile takes time and a lot of work to accomplish; you must be dedicated and persistent in order to achieve something you've never achieved before.

Once you decide to increase your financial IQ (Intelligent Quotient), how do you go about it? What are the necessary steps to be taken? The very fact that hundreds of thousands of people like Warren Buffet, Steve Jobs, Oprah Winfrey, and Ibrahim Alinco Dangote have done it and succeeded is ample proof that you can do it. Yes, you can! Many of these people in their early lives (when their unripe fruit is in the process of ripening) were termed dullards, dumb, nonentities, and other kinds of derogatory names. They simply talked to themselves more, and less to others.

Nurture your nature. "Everybody has talent, but ability takes hard work," once remarked Michael Jordan. I am curious about why the educational system does not provide financial education to students. Educators seem to think that money has some sort of quasi-religious or cult-like taint on it, believing that the love of money is the root of all evil. But is money the real root of all evil?

Money by itself is not evil – it is neutral. Money is just money. The majority of people are of the view that it is not the love of money that is evil, it is the lack of money that causes evil. Thus, it's the lack of financial education that causes people to do stupid things or be misled by stupid people. As you aspire to be at the top of the success ladder, you need to develop your Financial IQ. The rich and the poor have different money problems. Using Kiyosaki's views, my understanding of the money problems of the poor are:

- Not having enough money.
- Using credit to supplement money shortages.
- The rising cost of living.
- Paying more in taxes the more they make.
- Fear of emergencies.
- Bad financial advice.
- Not enough retirement money.

The money problems of the rich are:

- Having too much money.
- Needing to keep it safe and invested.
- Not knowing whether people like them or their money.
- Needing smarter financial advisors.
- Raising spoiled kids.
- Estate and inheritance planning.
- Excessive government taxes.

Money alone does not solve your money problems, and hard work does not solve money problems because the world is filled with hardworking people who have no money to show for it. Education does not solve money problems because the world is filled with highly educated people who are struggling financially, and a job doesn't solve money problems. Financial Intelligence solves money problems, according to experts. Some of the general money problems I have discovered during the course of writing this book include:

- I don't earn enough money.
- I'm deeply in debt.
- I cannot afford to buy a home.
- My car is broken but I have no money to fix it.
- My child wants to attend higher education, but I do not have the money to support them.
- I'm retired and I'm running out of money.

Financial acumen has the capacity to address and potentially resolve these and various financial issues. What then is this financial intelligence? Simply put, it is that part of our total intelligence we use to solve financial problems. If our financial intelligence is not developed enough to solve our problems, they persist – they don't go away. You need to be a problem-solver if you want to increase your financial intelligence because money problems make you smarter if you solve them.

Financial intelligence is that part of our intelligence we use to solve our financial problems, while Financial IQ is the measurement of that. In other words, Financial IQ is how we quantify our financial intelligence. For Robert T. Kiyosaki, there are five basic financial IQs:

1. Making more money.
2. Protecting your money.
3. Budgeting your money.
4. Leveraging your money.
5. Improving your financial information.

Asking the right question brings forth the correct answer. Now ask yourself: how do I increase my financial IQ? There are three basic parts of the human brain:

1. The left brain

2. The right brain

3. The subconscious mind

The left brain:

Generally, this part of the brain is used for reading, writing, speaking, and logic. Kids who do well in school have well-developed left brains. Some professions that belong to this group are: writers, scientists, lawyers, accountants, and schoolteachers.

The right brain:

This part of the brain is often associated with pictures, art, music, and other more non-linear relationships (creativity and imagination). Some professions in this group include: designers, architects, and musicians.

The subconscious mind:

For Robert, this is the most powerful of the three brains because it includes the "old brains," often called the primitive brain. It does not think, but rather reacts, fights, flees, or freezes.

So, which of the three brains control your money? To Robert, it is neither the left brain, right brain, nor the subconscious mind. Rather, it's the alignment, synchronization, and agreement between the powers of the three brains. Instead of the three brains working against each other, they work together. If a person could align and develop all three brains, they could have a greater chance of success in society.

Thinking Big, Starting Small

Rome was not built in a day. Picture the big picture but take small action consistently; some scholars call it "blue-sky thinking." You may have a plan for your future, visualize your D.C.A., set a deadline for its actualization but you have no money for sponsorship. How do you go about the money business? My sole concern here is to bring to the limelight some of the secrets of getting, saving, and investing money.

To advise a person to save money without describing *how* to save would be like drawing a picture of a horse and writing under it, "This is a horse." Advising someone to save money without providing guidance on how to save effectively is akin to stating the obvious without offering any practical assistance. Money is one of the essential materials you need as you ascend the ladder of success. Napoleon Hill explains that saving money is solely a matter of habit. Human beings, through the "law of habit," shape their own personality. Through repetition, any act indulged in a few times becomes a habit, and the mind appears to be nothing more than a mass of motivating forces growing out of our daily habits. This we can liken to the way we learned the road to our place of work, church, school, club, etcetera.

We are the victims of our habits, no matter who we are or what our life-calling may be. Any idea that is deliberately fixed in the mind or permitted to set itself up in the mind as a result of suggestion, environment, or the influence of associates is sure to cause us to indulge in acts that confirm the nature of the idea. Thus, form the habit of thinking and talking of prosperity and abundance, and very soon material evidence of these will begin to manifest itself in wider opportunity and new and unexpected opportunities. Like attracts like!

According to Hill, one of the most successful bankers in the state of Illinois has this sign hanging in his private office: "WE TALK AND THINK ONLY OF ABUNDANCE HERE. IF YOU HAVE A TALE OF WOE, PLEASE KEEP IT, AS WE DON'T WANT IT."

The poverty consciousness is formed from the habit of thinking of and fearing poverty, like Job expressing his immense suffering in the Bible by saying, "Lo! The thing I had feared has come upon me."

To untie yourself from the poverty consciousness, you have to overcome the fear of poverty. You must take two definite steps, provided you aren't in debt (the merciless master, and a fatal enemy of the habit of saving). Poverty alone is sufficient to kill ambition, destroy self-confidence, and destroy hope, but adding to it the burden of debt results in failure. You cannot do your best work, you cannot express yourself in terms that command respect, and you cannot create or carry out a definite purpose in life with heavy debt hanging over your head. The person who is bound in the slavery of debt is just as helpless as the slave who is bound by ignorance or by actual chains.

To master the fear of poverty, first quit the habit of buying on credit, and follow this by gradually paying off the debts you've already incurred. Any habit may be discontinued by building in its place some other and more desirable habit. The "spending" habit must be replaced by the "saving" habit to attain financial independence. To merely discontinue an undesirable habit isn't enough, as such habits tend to reappear unless the place they formerly occupied in the mind is filled by some other habit of a different nature. In other words, the discontinuance of a habit leaves a vacuum in the mind, and this hole must be filled up with some other form of habit or the old one will return and claim its place. In line with this, the Bible says, "When an unclean spirit goes out of a man it wanders through waterless country looking for a place to rest . . . I'll return to the home it came from. But on arrival, finding it unoccupied, swept, and tidied, it then goes off and collects seven other spirits more evil than itself and they go in and set up house there" (Matt.12:43-45).

The person without money is at the mercy of the person who has money! This is regardless of the amount of ability he may possess, the training he has had, or the genius he was gifted by nature. No wonder William Shakespeare remarks that:

> Neither a borrower, nor a lender be:
> For loan oft loses both itself and friend,
> And borrowing dulls the edge of husbanding.
> This above all: to thine ownself be true,
> And it must follow, as the night the day,
> Thou canst then be false to any man.

The question of how much one should save depends on many conditions, some of which may be within one's control and some of which may not. It's quite unfortunate that many have made a million dollars but haven't a cent. One cannot criticize a person for succeeding because they have the necessary knowledge. It would be unjust/unreasonable to criticize someone simply because they have achieved success. Success should be viewed as a result of someone's efforts, abilities, and perhaps even their understanding of how to navigate certain situation or opportunities. In reference to the importance of financial prudence, George S. Clason emphasizes that:

- For every ten coins you place within your purse, take out for use but nine. Your purse will start to fatten at once and its increasing weight will feel good in your hand and bring satisfaction to your soil.

- Budget your expenses so that you may have coins to pay for the necessities, to pay for your enjoyment, and to gratify your worthwhile desire without spending more than nine-tenths of your earnings.

- Put each coin to laboring that it may reproduce its kind even as the flocks of the field and help bring to the income, a stream wealth that shall flow constantly into your purse.

- Guard your treasure from loss by investing only where your principal is safe, where it may be reclaimed if desirable, and where you won't fail to collect a fair rental. Consult with wise men. Secure the advice of those experienced in the profitable handling of gold. Let their wisdom protect your treasure from unsafe investments.

- Make your dwelling a profitable investment.

- Provide in advance for the needs of your growing age and the protection of your family.

- Cultivate your own powers, study, become wiser to become more skillful, and respect yourself. Thus, increase the ability to earn.

Consider this anonymous proverbial/poetic expression: "A bag heavy with gold or a clay tablet carved with words of wisdom." If you're asked to make a choice, which would you choose? Many will go for the gold, while others will go for the words of wisdom. In support of your financial independence journey, there are principles and instructional guides you must abide by, which I learned while researching George S. Clason. They are called The Five Laws of Gold (which I choose to call the laws of money), and they include:

1. Gold comes gladly and in increasing quantity to any person who will put by not less than one-tenth of his earnings to create an estate for his future and that of his family.

2. Gold labors diligently and consistently for the wise owner who finds for its profitable employment, multiplying even as the flock of the field.

3. Gold changes to the protection of the cautious owner who invests it under the advice of wise men in its handling (which suggests that wealth becomes secure and grows when it is managed wisely and prudently).

4. Gold slips away from the person who invests it in business for purposes with which he's not familiar or which aren't approved by those skilled in its keep.

5. Gold flees the person who would force it to impossible earning, who follows the alluring advice of tricksters and schemers, or who trusts it to his own inexperience and romantic desires in investment.

To him who is without knowledge of the five laws, gold comes not often and goes away quickly. But to him who abides by the five laws, gold comes and works as his dutiful slave. Why not pay now to play tomorrow?

Takeaway from Chapter Six

▶ One of the major factors distracting people from making the sky their starting point is the low self-esteem or self-image they have created. To get rid of this, tell yourself that "old things shall pass away." Take the necessary actions.

▶ Do you know that wealth and riches are your birthright? You're an asset to yourself. Increase your financial intelligence and Financial IQ to make merriment of your God-given resources.

▶ Picture the big picture but always start small, for Rome wasn't built in a day. Untie yourself from the poverty consciousness and jump with your parachute.

CHAPTER SEVEN

Doing The Same Thing, Receiving the Same Result

"If a man is called to be a street sweeper, he should sweep streets as Michelangelo painted or Beethoven composed music, or Shakespeare writes poetry. He should sweep streets so well that all the hosts of heaven and earth will pause to say, 'here lived a great street sweeper who did his job well.'"

—Dr. Martin Luther King, Jr.

The Law of Cause and Effect

One of the things I love about my findings in philosophy is what is called the Principle of Causality, or that which brings about a certain effect. A cause produces an effect. For example, after planting seeds in fertile soil and watering them regularly, the gardener observes with satisfaction as tiny green sprouts emerge from the earth.

When the scripture says "whatever a man sows, that he also reaps" (Gal. 6:7-8), what does it really mean? When John Locke said, "I have always thought the actions of men the best interpreters of their thoughts," to what was he referring? When James Allen wrote "As a man thinketh," what was he trying to expurgate? Simply put, experts and scholars tell us that the effect that we are experiencing is a result of a cause – it has its hook on something; something is solidly responsible for it.

While explaining this concept, Brian Tracy (in *The Psychology of Selling*) tells a fantastic story (which I have summarized) that better explains the

Law of Cause and Effect. A young salesman seeks advice on improving his sales. Initially, he resists the suggestion to cut his long hair, believing it's irrelevant to his success. However, after reluctantly getting a haircut, he sees a significant increase in sales. As his success grows, he becomes complacent and allows his hair to grow long again, attributing his success solely to his product and personality. However, his sales decline once more, leading to financial struggles and a return to his parents' house.

Every effect is related to a cause. When this is applied to human conduct, great thinkers and philosophers (like Plato and Immanuel Kant) have called it the "Principle of Justice." All things (whether visible or invisible) are subservient to and fall within the scope of this infinite and eternal law of causation; the thoughts and deeds of men (whether secret or open) cannot escape it. No wonder James Allen rightly pointed out: "Do right, it recompenses; do wrong, the equal retribution must be made."

This perfect justice of cause and effect regulates human life and conduct (including every portion of the physical universe, from the speck of dust to the greatest sun). The truth is that people can and do choose what causes they set in operation, but they cannot change the nature of effects. In other words, they can decide what thoughts to think and what deeds to do but they can't control the results of those thoughts and deeds. People have all the power to act, but their power ends with the acts committed. The result of the act cannot be altered, annulled, or escaped – it's irrevocable.

The "problem of evil" subsists in people's own evil deeds, and it is solved when those deeds are purified. The French philosopher Jean-Jacques Rousseau once said, "Man, seek no longer the origin of evil; thou thyself art its origin." Effect can never be divorced from cause; it can never be of a different nature from nature. On this, Emerson remarked that, "Justice isn't postponed, a perfect equity adjusts the balance in all parts of life."

As the fruit to the tree and the water to the spring, so is cause to effect. Go into the fields and country lanes in the springtime, and you'll see farmers and gardeners busy sowing seeds in the newly prepared soil. If you were to ask any one of those gardeners or farmers what kind of produce they expected from the seed they were sowing, they would doubtless regard you as foolish and would tell you that they do not expect at all and that it is a matter of common knowledge that their produce will be the kind he's sowing, and that he is sowing wheat, or barley, or turnips (as the case may be).

All the parables of Jesus Christ are illustrative of this truth and are drawn from the simple facts of nature. There's a process of seed-sowing in the mind and life, a spiritual sowing that leads to a harvest according to the kind of seed sown. Thoughts, words, and acts are seeds sown, and by the inviolable law of things (the justice of cause and effect), they produce after their kind. The person who thinks hateful thoughts brings hatred upon himself, while the person who thinks loving thoughts is loved. The person who sows wrong thoughts and deeds, and prays that God will bless them, is in the position of a farmer who, having sown weeds, asks God to bring forth harvest of wheat. That which you sow, you reap.

James Allens said, "I once heard a preacher pray very earnestly for forgiveness, and shortly afterwards, in the course of his sermon, he called upon his congregation to show no mercy to the enemies of the church." People believe they can sow the seed of strife, impurity, and unbrotherliness and then gather in a rich harvest of peace, purity, and concord by merely asking for it. What a pathetic absurdity in human conception!

In line with the law of cause and effect, the Indian statesman Mahatma Gandhi once said that "in a gentle way, you can shake the world." Believing in that maxim, I have made it a point of duty to pray silently in my heart to the Infinite Intelligence God during holy mass after the holy communion: "Father, let me see and show real love to people and let people also see and show real love to me." The good thing about this prayer is that I have received real love from people in school, grocery stores, churches, and even the office.

Be aware that cause results in effect and thoughts result in your character, circumstances, health and body, purpose, and especially in your achievements. Change your thought content and master your circumstances. Dreamers are the saviors of the world.

People aren't Rational, but...

To say that man isn't rational (either by nature, or not) is to engage in a mind-battle (or argument) with philosophers. It may be like the battle between the rationalists (those who are of the view that all human knowledge is derived solely from reason, excluding sense-perception) and the empiricists (those who believe that all human knowledge is solely from the senses and not from reason).

As you can't do a good deal with a bad partner, so also you may not be able to climb to the top without knowing how to manipulate people.

The concept of "manipulation" stirs our curiosity. Can manipulation be used negatively? To understand manipulation, one should know the difference between "to manipulate" and "to manage." You generally manage things or situations that are simple, constant, and don't change while you manipulate things/situations that respond and react, change, and are variable and more complex. For instance, when you work for long hours and get a salary at the end of the month (or bi-weekly), you manage your finances. But when you invest and others work for you, you manipulate your finances. When you deposit your savings in the bank, you manage them, but when you invest them in the stock market, you manipulate them. Thus, manipulation is skillful management.

Manipulation simply signifies the artful use of knowledge. Think of what happens between parents and children. Consider a parent who wants their child to excel academically. The parent notices that the child is not putting enough effort into their studies. To motivate the child, the parent might employ manipulation by saying, "If you don't get good grades, you won't be able to go to your favorite college, and then you will end up with a terrible job and no money." By instilling fear about the future, the parent manipulates the child into studying harder to avoid the perceived negative consequences.

Is there any need to manipulate people? I think it is relative. Once, a man came to see a psychologist. He told him that he recently had surgery on his stomach. During the operation the doctors had by mistake left two mosquitoes in his stomach. The mosquitoes flew around in his stomach all night making a *buzzzz* sound and didn't let him sleep. He further told him that he had visited many doctors but all of them had laughed at him and called him a clown.

The psychologist told him that he dealt only with such problems so he had come to the right person. He asked the man to lie down, checked his stomach, and confirmed the existence of two mosquitoes. The man was overjoyed at hearing this. Afterwards, the psychologist asked him to come the following Sunday morning. The man did come, and the psychologist hypnotized him, went to another room, caught two mosquitoes, put them into a transparent box, came back to the room, de-hypnotized him, and showed him the box. The man immediately fell on his feet. He thanked the psychologist profusely and said that at least now he would be able to sleep.

But before leaving, he requested the psychologist hand over the box to him. He said, "I will go to those so-called doctors who laughed at me and show them these mosquitoes."

Think about this for a moment and answer this question: were the actions performed by the psychologist not manipulation? It might not be wrong, after all, to say that manipulating people is sometimes required for personal success. Three things, according to Prabbal Frank, are needed to learn how to manipulate people. They include:

1. To understand what is to be done.
2. To know how to do it.
3. To actually do it.

In learning how to manipulate people, consider these tips:

- Learn to act, and don't react.
- Convince them with written materials.
- Allow others to blow your trumpet.
- Attract with gifts.
- People are better led than driven.
- Become their hero.
- Learn to say thank you.
- Appeal to peoples' self-interest.

Learn to act, and don't react:

It was D. Liard who once said, "Use your head to deal with yourself but use your heart to deal with others." Manipulating people starts with the manipulation of oneself. To manipulate oneself, learn to act and not react. Do you act or react? Are you in control of yourself or do others control you? As Ethel Barrymore once commented, "The best time to make friends is before you need them," so the best time for you to act is before you react. The majority of people react rather than act. If you react, then you let others control you, likely allowing them to influence your actions and make decisions for you, but when you act, you're totally in control of yourself.

Jesus Christ admonishes followers and believers that if a brother slaps you on one cheek, turn the other for him (Lk. 6:28-29). What does that imply? Should we act or react? It is a conscious choice to do something based on your principles when you act; a choice that makes you become powerful.

Convince them with written materials:

Prabbal was of the opinion that people tend to believe whatever is written and do not give that much credibility to something that is merely spoken. For example, if you go around telling people that if you go to XYZ location, you will get $100 as a gift from God, how many people do you think would really believe you? Perhaps only a few. But if you show them a newspaper stating the same fact, the majority of them will rush to that place.

Allow others to blow your trumpet:

How do you think people will feel if you only discuss matters that benefit you? Imagine Arnold Schwarzenegger or Jet Li standing in front of the audience and asking them to clap for them, as they are legends in the movie industry. People would be skeptical and feel they are eccentric. But compare that to when someone else praises you. People would shower you with adulation and echoes of thunderous claps.

Attract with gifts:

A man once went to a grocery shop and purchased some butter. While he was coming back, he happened to see the word "free" printed on the cover of the product. He immediately went back to the shop and asked the shopkeeper to give him the free article that came with the butter. The shopkeeper replied that there was no such thing. The man got angry, took the butter out, and told the shopkeeper, "See, it says cholesterol free."

The word "free" is such an attraction; it is a very powerful word but surprisingly, nothing is actually free. To convince people easily, make it a principle to give something free (something that costs you little but gives perceived value in the eyes of the customer) and watch how your product sale increases.

People are better led than driven:

It is very difficult to carry out or initiate a new order of things; it's even more difficult to drive people than to lead them, because you must have a tough mind and a tender heart, as seen in Jesus Christ's teaching, "be ye therefore wise as serpents and harmless as doves" (Matt. 10:16), where he blends the toughness of the serpent and the softness of the dove. Great leaders do not wait for followers to come; they do not seek the approval of people before starting on any path (their journey to the unknown island), they just go ahead, and gradually like-minded people join them.

Become their hero:

In life, you're either influenced by somebody or you're influencing people. People dream of becoming their ideal hero and heroine. Prabbal Frank suggests that a person's admiration for specific figures reflects their underlying values and aspirations. According to him, admiration for figures like Mahatma Gandhi or Mother Teresa indicates a love for benevolence and philanthropy. Admiration for wealthy figures like Bill Gates or Rockefeller signifies a desire for wealth. Admiring celebrities such as Amitabh Bachchan or Arnold Schwarzenegger shows a yearning for recognition.

Those who admire sports figures like Don Bradman or Andre Agassi are lovers of sports. Admiring thinkers like Swami Dayanand suggests good thinking skills, and admiration for historical figures known for power, like Hitler or Napoleon, indicates a pursuit of power.

Learn to say thank you:

There are three things that change a person (I learned them from one of my senior secondary school teachers) and they are:

1. Thank you.
2. Please.
3. I'm sorry.

My priority is "thank you." Those two words are simply words of appreciation. People like to be appreciated. This, in psychology, is called "reinforcement." Learn to say thank you, as being grateful or appreciative does not seem to come naturally for many people. Learn to have an attitude of gratitude by beginning to incorporate it into your daily life.

Appeal to peoples' self-interest:

Robert Greene, in *The 48 Laws of Power*, was of the opinion that if you need to turn on an ally for help, don't bother to remind him of your past assistance and good deeds (for he will find a way to ignore you); instead, uncover something in your request or in your alliance with him that will benefit him, and emphasize it out of all proportion. He will respond enthusiastically when he sees something to be gained. In your quest for power and becoming a success, you will constantly find yourself in the position of asking for help from those more powerful than you (those already at the top). There is an art to asking for help, an art that depends on your ability to understand the person you're dealing with, and to not confuse your needs with theirs. The secret is: appeal to their self-interest.

How may I Serve, please?

Often, I hear that leadership is a call to service. But the primordial question is: what kind of leadership and service is it? Jesus Christ made it so clear when the other ten apostles were indignant at the two sons of Zebedee requesting to be seated at God's left and right hand at His kingdom. He called them and said, "No, anyone who wants to be great among you must be your servant" (Matt. 20:24-28).

Greg Reid, author of *Three Feet from Gold,* told a story of how surprised he was at the readiness of the world superstars to "pass it on," even while they were still actively engaged in their own endeavors. In chapter six (Formulating Success) of that book, he narrated his encounter with Jack Mates, who startled him by saying, "How may I serve you?" In the view of Jack Mates, he retorted that he did not see himself as a hero but more of a patriot who had done his part to serve his country and the greater cause.

As you aspire to the ladder of success, there is one interesting thing you should put into your basket of knowledge: **pleasing personality.**

Personality is the sum total of your characteristics and appearance that distinguishes you from all others. The clothes you wear, the lines in your face, the tone of your voice, the thoughts you think, the character you have developed by those thoughts – all these constitute part of your personality. The style of your clothes and their appropriateness, and the manner in which you shake hands, forms an important part of your personality, going a long way in attracting or repelling those with whom you shake hands.

Taking a keen-hearted interest in people is one sure way you can express the composite of your personality that will always attract them. Brian Tracy emphasized this pleasing or attractive personality in his book *The Psychology of Selling.* He threw light on dressing for success, hair care, and shaking hands firmly; your success in any endeavor depends on how pleasant and attractive your personality is. Have the interest of your prospect at heart. Human beings will likely listen with intense interest to those who have the tact to talk to them about what lies closest to their hearts. There is something about a person's personality that cannot be captured by the photographer or artist; it is not capable of description. One of the reasons, in the view of Dr. Sidney Newton Bremer, that so many fail to get what they want out of life is that their personalities repel rather than attract. Personality is not something you can turn on and off like a light switch or dab on like lipstick or powder; it goes beyond physical appearance.

We are not born with a pleasing personality; it is not an inheritable trait, and it must be cultivated through social intercourse. Developing a pleasing personality starts with the foundation of a sound, positive character. You may embellish yourself with clothes of the latest design and conduct yourself a pleasing manner as far as outside appearances go but if there's greed, envy, hatred, jealousy, avarice, and selfishness in your heart, you will never attract anyone, except those characters that harmonize with your own; those who are attracted to you are those whose inward natures parallel your own.

In the opinion of Napoleon Hill, you may embellish yourself with an artificial smile that belies your feelings, and you may practice the art of hand-shaking to imitate perfectly the handshake of someone who is an adept at this art. But if these outward manifestations of an "attractive personality" lack that vital factor called "earnestness of purpose," they will repel instead of attract. To develop an attractive personality, make it a point of duty to familiarize yourself with these six factors:

1. Form the habit of being interested in other people and make it your business to find their good qualities and speak of them with praise.

2. Develop the ability to speak with force and conviction, both in your ordinary conversational tones and before public gatherings where you must use more volume.

3. Clothe yourself in a style that is becoming to your physical build and the work you are engaged in.

4. Develop a positive character through the aid of building rigid self-discipline and self-control.

5. Learn to shake hands so you express warmth of feeling and enthusiasm.

6. Attract other people to you by first "attracting yourself" to them.

Takeaway from Chapter Seven

▶ Nothing is permanent in life. The only thing that is permanent, as philosophers proffer, is change. Because of the chasm of change in life, master the inner cause of your life to control the effect.

▶ You can only control the cause; you cannot take control of the effect because whatever you sow, you reap.

▶ It has been proven beyond reasonable doubt that success in life, to a large extent, depends on people. So, to find your way through the ladder of success, appeal to people's self-interest, because people are not rational but emotional.

▶ To get right to people's emotional status quo, there are certain skills you need to know. Always say thank you whenever you receive favor from people. Lead, but never drive people.

▶ If you cannot do a great thing, you can do a small thing in a great way. Greatness starts with the right intention to serve others. Remember, whoever wants to be great amongst you must be your slave, as learned from the Bible.

CHAPTER EIGHT

Across The Bridge

"You're the same today as you'll be in five years except for two things: the books you read and the people you meet."

—Charlie "Tremendous" Jones

The Driving Force of the Masterminders

Why is it that Jesus Christ, immediately after the temptation in the wilderness, began to call his disciples? Why is it that He went for only twelve disciples and not more or less? Why is it that upon His divinity (though He came on earth in His humanity), He still was in search of partners (Matt. 4:18-22)? The need for "allied force" answers these questions as seen in the transfiguration (the supra-perceptive communication of Jesus Christ with Moses and Elijah) of the Messiah (Matt. 17:1-6).

The American self-made millionaire and successful author Jim Rohn says, "You're the average of the five people you spend the most time with." Why are parents always telling their kids that they don't want them hanging out with "those kids?" Can you remember your parents telling you to stop mingling with a certain group of pals? This is because we know that kids (and even adults) become like the people they hang out with. Thus, it is pertinent that you spend time with the people you want to become like. In other words, if you really want to be successful, you've got to start spending time with successful people.

As Mike Murdock puts it, "Pay any price to stay in the presence of extraordinary people." This maxim was truly relevant in the life of John Assaraf. John was a street kid who had been entangled in the world of drugs and gangs but later turned around by constantly listening to successful businessmen tell their stories of success and failure. They taught John never to give up on his dream. "No matter what that failure," they told him, "try another way; go up, over, around, or through, but never give up, for there's always a way."

In his book *How to Get What You Want*, Dr. Sydney Newton Bremer shares a fantastic and dazzling story. A young man, with only three months of formal education, had an idea. He was twenty-nine. The year was 1876 and the man's name was Thomas Alva Edison. Edison knew he had a deficiency that he would need to overcome if he were ever to be a success in life. He recognized that his lack of even a first-grade education was a handicap. "In my desire for success, why can't I use the brains of other people?" he reasoned. He said, "I will pool the talents of chemists, engineers, modelmakers, scientists, mathematicians, and skilled mechanics –sixty-one men in all – and we will plan on a minor invention every ten days, and a major invention every six months." The idea worked. In less than six years he had more than 300 patents. He didn't stop there but went on to become the greatest inventor the world has ever known, inventing the electric light bulb we are enjoying today.

Being virtuous sets you free from anxiety, being wise sets you free from perplexity, and being brave sets you free from fear.

From Edison, an idea was born that is now recognized as the "Mastermind Alliance." Andrew Carnegie knew little or nothing about the manufacture of steel; rather, he was a genius for organizing men. He surrounded himself with men who knew all there was to be known about steelmaking, finance, law, chemistry, physics, marketing, and economics. He organized them into a management circle, which became the "mastermind" of his organization. Together they worked in a spirit of perfect harmony, in a single common effort or goal. They all worked like a **TEAM** – Together Each Achieve More. Together they all became rich.

Power is essential for success in the accumulation of money. Plans are inert and useless without sufficient power to translate them into action. Power, in the words of Napoleon Hill, is an organized and intelligently directed knowledge. Power, as used here, refers to "organized effort." This is produced through the coordination of effort of two or more people who work toward a definite end in a spirit of harmony. Since power is organized knowledge, its sources of accumulation include:

- Infinite intelligence that is accessed with the aid of creative imagination.
- Accumulated experience (or that portion of it that has been organized and recorded) may be found in any well-equipped public library and may be taught in schools, colleges, and universities.
- Experiment and research.

On examining the three major sources of human knowledge (as outlined above), it becomes apparent the difficulty people would have if they depended on their efforts alone in assembling knowledge and expressing it through definite plans in terms of actions. Thus, if their plans are comprehensive (and if they contemplate large proportions), they must induce others to cooperate with them before they can inject the necessary element of power. True success comes by producing values that are of service to others, and not by climbing over them.

The principle of the Masterminders entails coordination of knowledge and effort, in a spirit of harmony, between two or more people, for the attainment of a definite purpose. According to Napoleon Hill, there are two characteristics of the Mastermind principle:

1. Economic phase
2. Psychic phase

The Economic phase: Economic advantages may be created by people who surround themselves with the advice, counsel, and personal cooperation of a group of people who are willing to lend them wholehearted aid in a spirit of perfect harmony. This form of cooperative alliance has been the basis of nearly every great fortune.

The Psychic phase: This may sound abstract, and much more difficult to comprehend or unravel, because it refers to the spiritual forces with which humans are well acquainted. Napoleon Hill says that "no two minds ever come together without thereby a creation of a third, invisible, intangible force which may be likened to a third mind."

There are only known two elements in the whole universe – energy and matter. Matter may be broken down into units of molecules, atoms, and electrons. There are units of matter that may be isolated, separated, and analyzed; so also, there are units of energy. Thus, the human mind is a form of energy, a part of it being spiritual in nature. When the minds of two people are coordinated in a spirit harmony, the spiritual units of energy of each mind form an affinity, which we can say constitute the "psychic" phase of the Mastermind.

It is common knowledge that a group of electric batteries will provide more energy than a single battery. An individual battery will provide energy in proportion to the number and capacity of the cells it contains. The human brain functions in a similar fashion, even though some brains are more efficient than others, so a group of brains coordinated (or connected) in a spirit of harmony will provide more thought-energy than a single brain, just as a group of electric batteries will provide more energy than a single battery. This was vividly exposed in the book *Three Feet from Gold* (in chapter ten), by Buckland.

Greg was able to acquire some success tips, which include:

- Any new business venture takes patience. It often takes three, four, or sometimes five years to discover whether you're a hero or an idiot. But on the right side, there will always be someone there to tell you either way.

- The margin between success and failure is a very thin line. History is the past so base decisions on the future.

- Be prepared for NO. Your degree of success in anything you choose is in proportion to how many rejections you can sustain. The number of nos you're willing to go through to get the desired result will dictate whether you succeed or fail.

- You don't need a wall full of plaques and degrees to become successful in this world. But you do need to watch and follow the action steps of what successful people do.

- Live each day by this principle as composed by James Owen:

Live each day with courage.
Take pride in your work.
Always finish what you start.
Do what has to be done.
Be tough, but fair.
When you make a promise, keep it.
Ride for the brand.
Talk less, say more.

Remember that some things aren't for sale. Know where to draw the line. Here are some personal recommendations for you:

Step 1

Make a list of everyone you spend time with on a regular basis – your family members, coworkers, neighbors, friends, people in your civic organization, and fellow members of your religious group.

Step 2

When you have completed your list, go back and put a minus sign (-) next to those people who are negative and toxic, and a plus sign (+) next to those who are positive and nurturing. As you decide about each person, you might find that a pattern will begin to form. Stop spending time with those people with a minus sign next to their name. If that is impossible (remember, nothing is impossible; it's always a choice), then severely decrease the amount of time you spend with them. Think about it. I'm sure you know people who only drain you of your energy, complain a lot about others, and blame others for their circumstances whenever you are around them. They're nothing but vampires!

I tell you solemnly, stop spending your time with them. You're better off spending time alone than spending time with people who will hold you back with their victim mentality and mediocre standards. Surround yourself with possibility thinkers, idealists, and visionaries. If you're going to be successful, you have to start hanging out with successful people; they could share their success strategies with you. Try them and see if they fit. Experiment with doing what they do, reading what they read, thinking the way they think.

In the course of spending time with my masterminders, I've discovered my own Masterminder formula: Mostly spend your time with people who are more successful than you; sometimes spend your time with people who are at the same level/status as you; and at lastly, spend less time with people who are below your level. Each category of people has something to teach you.

Am I Made to Succeed?

Some people are born with golden and silver spoons, while others are born with wooden spoons. What really matters is what you do with that spoon at the end of the day. Some people are born into a well-to-do family, some are born with a good physique and stature, while the "unfortunate ones" are handicapped. Some are born to be tall while others are born to be short.

The number-one yardstick, benchmark, and primordial factor in the attainment of success is Positive Mental Attitude (PMA). In Napoleon Hill's views, if you begin to apply the principles associated with PMA, you are assured of accomplishing your successful endeavor, you are on the right track and headed in the right direction toward getting what you want. Thus, PMA is the catalyst that makes any combination of success principles work to attain a worthwhile end.

However, one of the reasons many people regard themselves as being unfortunate in life is as a result of what Napoleon Hill called "NMA – Negative Mental Attitude." This simply means a person's mindset being characterized by pessimism, negativity, and a general lack of enthusiasm or hope. The truth is that if you think that you are among the unfortunate ones, you know what? The world has given you a raw deal. If you're unhappy with your world and really want to change it, the right place to start is with yourself. "If you're right," said Napoleon Hill, "your world will be right."

One of the important techniques for changing your world is to identify yourself with an image that will inspire you to make the right decisions and have a DCA. It has been proven beyond all reasonable doubt that every human being is born a genius – it's in YOU. You're a success.

Life never leaves us stranded. If life hands us a problem, it also hands us the abilities to meet the problem, for God who has given a person a big head will provide him with a proportionate neck for carrying it. Our abilities vary as we are motivated to use them.

Milo C. Jones, as quoted by Hill and Stone, hadn't tried to acquire wealth when he had good health. And then he became sick. When he became sick, the odds were stacked heavily against him. When Jones was in good health, he worked very hard. He was a farmer, and he operated a small farm near Fort Atkinson, Wisconsin. But somehow he seemed unable to make his farm yield much more than the bare necessities for himself and his family. This kind of existence went on year after year. Then, suddenly something happened!

Jones was stricken with extensive paralysis and confined to his bed. He was completely incapacitated, barely able to move his body. His relatives thought he would permanently be unhappy. But guess what? Milo turned the whole situation around. Recognizing that his body was incapacitated, Milo used his mind (the greatest asset to every human being). Yes, his body was paralyzed, but his mind was unaffected. First, Jones counted his blessings. He discovered that he had so very much for which to be thankful, thereby going into "mental action" and revealing to his family his plans. He said, "I'm no longer able to work with my hands, so I've decided to work with my mind. Every one of you can, if you will take the place of my hands, feet, and physical body. Let's plant every tillable acre of our farm in corn. Then let's raise pigs and feed them the corn. Let's slaughter the pigs while they're young and tender and convert them into sausages. And then we can package them under a brand name and sell them in retail stores all over the country. They will sell like hotcakes."

Of course, they did sell like hotcakes! In a few years, the brand "Jones' Little Pig Sausages" became a household name. Isn't that incredible?

From my research, some of the likely excuses people may use, which act as "the mighty wall of Jericho," preventing them from achieving success, include:

- I have the wrong type of personality.
- I'm too poor to progress.
- I'm physically handicapped.
- I give up because I have tried it several times before and have failed.
- I belong to an inferior social group.
- I'm female.
- I'm not intelligent.
- Experts have predicted that my work will take me nowhere.
- I'm too young.
- I'm too old.

I have the wrong type of personality:

Many people have assumed that they can't progress in any sphere of human endeavor because they were born with the wrong personality. People have different types of personalities: introverts and extroverts; and four temperaments: sanguine, phlegmatic, choleric, and melancholic. Each of these has its different characteristics, strengths, and weaknesses. Becoming aware of these personalities and temperaments helps you put effort into working on areas of weakness in order to succeed.

We need to understand, according to Sumbye Kapena, that an inclination isn't an indictment. Thus, just because you're inclined to a certain weakness doesn't mean that you must necessarily fall prey to it. It means that the weakness needs two things: effort and prayer.

There is ample evidence from many world-renowned people that you can indeed get rid of your weaknesses, thereby enhancing your strengths. Here are a few examples:

- **Socrates** – According to psychologist Zophyrus, Socrates had many natural weaknesses (that he himself admitted to) that he refused to give in to, conquering them with the continual practice of virtue.

- *John Fitzgerald Kennedy* – Before the death of Joe Kennedy (his elder brother), JFK was a shy and a timid person. He worked on this when he recognized he was going for political leadership. He became an outgoing public speaker and the President of the USA in 1961.

I'm too poor to progress:

Some people convince themselves that just because they are without money and material wealth, they can't progress in life. Stop! That is wrong thinking. If you are poor, this may be just a situational fact of life. You need not be ashamed of it. If it was due to some mistakes on your part, acknowledge it and determine never to repeat them. Some world-renowned personalities came from a poor background:

- *Aesop* – Once a slave, he later came to be a world-renowned philosopher.

- *Shakespeare* – His father was a butcher and a grazer, yet he went on to become a well-known author and poet.

- *Ben Carson* – His mother, an African-American, worked as a housemaid yet Ben became a world-renowned neurosurgeon (best known for his delicate operations to separate Siamese twins (who are born stuck to each other).

I'm physically handicapped:

There is a big difference between "born handicapped" and "I'm handicapped." Being physically handicapped is a limitation that shouldn't be underrated. It worsens when one wallows in self-pity. People who are physically disabled have gone on to be successful in life. Some of them include:

- *Helen Adams Keller* – Born blind and deaf, she graduated from university in 1904 and later became a lecturer and an author.

- *Franklin Delano Roosevelt* – Confined to wheelchair, he went on to become the President of the United States of America (1933-1945).

- *Napoleon Bonaparte and Julius Caesar* – History says that these men were epileptics (suffering from seizures), yet they became great generals and statesmen.

I give up because I've tried several times before and have failed:

Some people take the number of times they have failed in a certain endeavor to mean that they will never make it. Each failure draws you nearer to the solution as long as you do not repeat the mistakes. Some world personalities who didn't give up after encountering failure include:

- *Abraham Lincoln* – This "giant" had a long series of attempts; some turned out to be a success, while others didn't before he was finally elected President of the United States of America.

- *Ernest Miller Hemingway* – He was made to review his manuscript for *The Old Man and the Sea* eighty times before it was finally accepted for publishing.

I belong to an inferior social group:

Some people, said Kapena, used the social grouping they belong to such as their continent, country, or tribe as an excuse for their lack of progress. Truthfully speaking, we are all created equally by God. Some worlds personalities who fought inequality and discrimination include:

- *William Wilberforce* – A prominent English evangelical and philanthropist who contributed to the abolition of the slave trade.

- *Martin Luther King* – An African American human rights activist who did a lot to teach the people of the United States to live as one, regardless of the color of their skin. His teaching is well summarized in his popular speech "I Have a Dream," presented in August 1963.

- *Nelson Mandela* – He is one of the people who were at the forefront in the fight against apartheid (a policy where Black people were discriminated against by the whites). As a result, he was jailed for twenty-seven years.

I'm female:

It is a well-known fact that in the past, women and girls have been deprived of opportunities that were readily available to men and boys. That notwithstanding, many women in history have made their marks regardless, including:

- *Marie Curie* – A well-known scientist who discovered radium (along with her husband).

- *Margaret Thatcher* – The first female prime minister the United Kingdom. Her firmness earned her the name "Iron Lady."

I'm not intelligent:

Some people go around convinced that they're not intelligent. Usually, at one point in their life they were told that they weren't. Some world personalities who some time in their early lives were deemed to be unintelligent (even intellectually disabled), but who later became prominent figures include:

- *Albert Einstein* – He wasn't able to speak until the age of four, which made his parents fear that he was developmentally delayed. At the age of ten, his German schoolmaster told him, "You will never amount to much," yet Einstein went on to become one of the world-renowned mathematicians and scientists of the 20th century.

- *Sir Isaac Newton* – In his early years of school, he was always at the bottom of the class, yet he later became one of the world's known scientists and mathematicians.

- *Sigmund Freud* – Even his father (Jacob Freud) observed, "This boy will come to nothing," yet he later became one of the greatest psychologists of all time.

Experts have predicted that my work will take me nowhere:

Some people have been told by experts in their area of specialization that they are not up to the standard, and that it will therefore take them nowhere. This usually occurs when a person is trying to move away from the camp of mediocrity. However, experts have been proven wrong many times, like in these examples:

- *Wolfgang Amadeus Mozart* – This Austrian composer's music was criticized in his early years by the Emperor Ferdinand, saying that it was, "far too noisy, my dear Mozart, far too many notes." Yet his music is respected worldwide now.

- *Elvis Aaron Presley* – This American singer was fired by Jim Denny (manager of the Grand Ole Opry) who said, "You aren't going anywhere . . . you ought to go back to driving a truck." Yet, he later became a legend in his lifetime, the king of rock and roll.

I'm too young:

When you say you're too young for some opportunity to progress, you should give specific reasons. It's a pity that people let opportunities pass by because they feel they're too young. Some people who suceeded while they were still young include:

- *George Frederick Handel* – This renowned musician (composer of the internationally acclaimed "Hallelujah Chorus") started composing world famous music at the age of six and could play at least three musical instruments.

- *Wolfgang Amadeus Mozart* – He learned to play clavier (an early form of piano) at the age of four. At five, he learned to play violin and to read and write music. When he was six, he started composing music and performing before large crowds of people.

- *Galileo Galilei* – This Italian astronomer and physicist was nine years old when he discovered the principle of the pendulum in the swinging lamp in the Cathedral of Pisa.

I'm too old:

When you say that you're too old, you should be specific about what you're too old to do. When you're specific, you'll identify things that you can't do at your age and things that you actually can do but that you're just trying to run away from. Some well-known people who lived useful lives even at an advanced age include:

- *Cato* – This philosopher taught himself Greek when he was eighty years old.

- *Noah Webster* – This American lexicographer and philologist started work on yet another dictionary at the age of eighty-four.

- *Michelangelo Buonarroti* – At the ripe old age of ninety, this great Italian sculptor, painter, architect, and poet was still painting masterpieces.

I dare you! Memorize this formula to help you change your mindset and change your world: what the mind can conceive and believe, the mind can achieve with PMA. When it becomes part of you, you dare to aim higher. You're created to succeed!

Takeaway from Chapter Eight

▶ Many people have taken measures and means to attain their life goals. The easiest way to speak the language of the geniuses is to join the Masterminders.

▶ In the Mastermind Alliance, the underlying force there is that a perfect harmony must exist between you and those you are involved with.

▶ You are what you read and who you follow. Mind the kind of people you spend most of your time with: are they drainers or are they inspirers?

▶ Research proves that the three means by which one can accumulate knowledge include: infinite intelligence, accumulated experience, and experiment and research.

▶ The Mastermind alliance is comprised of an economic phase and a psychic phase.

▶ It has been proven beyond all reasonable doubt that whatever the mind of a person conceives and believes, it can achieve.

▶ Success is every person's birthright. You're born a success and made to succeed. Don't put any limitation before you if you doubt this; inquire from history. You were born a champion!

PART THREE
ACTION PLEASE!

CHAPTER NINE

Stop Planning, Take Action

"Many people die with their music still in them. Why is this so? Too often it's because they're always getting ready to live; before they know it, time runs out."

—Oliver Wendell Holmes

Back to the Drawing board

A man who meets a guru on the road asks: which way is success? The bearded sage doesn't speak but instead points to a place off in the distance. Thrilled by the prospect of quick and easy success, the man rushes off in the appropriate direction. Splat – he trips over and falls to the ground! He limps back, bruised and stunned, assuming he must have misinterpreted the message. He repeats his question to the guru, who for the second time, points silently in the same direction. Obediently, he walks off once more.

This time the splat is deafening, and when he crawls back, he is bloody, broken, and irate. Thus, he screams at the guru: "I asked you which way is success; I followed the direction you indicated and all I got were splatters. No more of this pointing, talk!"

Only then does the guru speak, saying, "Success is that way; just a little after that splat."

It is as clear as snow that life is made up of ups and downs and forward and backward movements. All of us at one time or another have experienced "the splat." But the difference lies in what we do after the splat. In the opinion of scholars, many times this is what separates high achievers from non-achievers. Ask yourself: "what do I do after the splat?" Do you stop after encountering the first difficulty? Or do you stop after encountering the second, third, and fourth, difficulties?

In the Bible there was an encounter between Jesus Christ and the Canaanite woman that went thus:

"Then came out a Canaanite woman from that district and started shouting: sir, son of David, take pity on me; my daughter is tormented by a devil . . . He said in reply, I was sent only to the lost sheep of the House of Israel . . . It's not fair to take the children's food and throw it to the house dogs. She retorted, ah yes, sir; but even house dogs can eat the scraps that fall from their master's table. Then Jesus answered her: woman, you have great faith; let your wish be granted" (Matt.15:21-28).

What is the takeaway from that narrative? Persistence! It is simply because of the persistent nature of the Canaanite woman that she was able to get her wish. Persistence is required for whatever you want to accomplish in life. Rick Mears (the champion racer) said that "to finish first, you must first finish."

Do you want to accomplish something in life? Be like the stonecutter who, according to Jacob Riis, persisted with over a hundred blows until the stone split into two. All things came to those who persistently go after them. Persistence and perseverance are the result of a strong will; stubbornness is the result of a strong will. Victory always comes to the most preserving. It is a secret of the ages that persistent people begin their success where most others quit. Many times, success consists of hanging on one minute longer. Pressing on has solved and always will solve the problems of the human race.

In a story told by John Mason, there were two men shipwrecked on an island. The minute they got onto the island one of them started screaming and yelling, "We're going to die! We're going to die! There's no food! No water! We're going to die!" The second man was propped up against a palm tree and acting so calm it drove the first man crazy. "Don't you understand?" We're going to die!" said the first man.

The second man said, "You don't understand, I make $100, 000 a week." The first man, dumbfounded, looked at him and asked, "What difference does that make? We're on an island with no food and no water, we're going to die!!"

The second man answered: "I make $100, 000 a week, and I tithe ten percent; my pastor will find me."

This story depicts one thing: when you're persistent, you know it, and so does everyone else. In Christopher Morley's words, "Big shots are only little shots that keep shooting." Failure is to wait at the path of least persistence. You have to be definite in what you want and stay on course, no matter what. The longer you hang in there, the greater the chance that something will happen in your favor. It's not going to be easy, but I strongly believe that whatever doesn't kill you will make you stronger. History has shown that despite the heartbreaking obstacles most notable winners encountered they still triumphed. They won because they refused to become discouraged by their defects. Fall down seven times and get up eight times, because **no** is a word on your path to **yes**, so do not give up too soon.

Consider this:

- Admiral Robert Peary attempted to reach the North Pole seven times before he made it on try number eight.

- In its first twenty-eight attempts to send rockets into space, NASA had twenty failures.

- Tawni O'Dell's career as a writer is a testament to her perseverance. After thirteen years, she had written six unpublished novels and collected 300 rejection slips. Finally, her first novel, *Back Roads*, was published in January 2000. Oprah Winfrey chose her book for the Oprah's Book Club, and the newly anointed novel rose to number two on the *New York Times* bestseller list (where it remained for eight weeks).

You've got to **Just Press On**. In 1895, America was in the grip of a terrible depression. A man living in the Midwest who lost his hotel decided to write a book to motivate and inspire others to persist and carry on in spite of the difficulties facing the nation. His name was Orison Swett Marden.

He took a room above a livery stable and for an entire year he worked night and day writing a book, which he entitled *Pushing to the Front*. Late one evening, he finally finished the last page of his book and, being tired and hungry, he went down the street to a small café for dinner. While he was away for an hour, the livery stable caught on fire. By the time he got back, his entire manuscript, more than eight hundred pages, had been destroyed by the flames.

Nonetheless, drawing on his inner resources, he sat down and spent another year writing the book over again. When the book was finished, he offered it to various publishers, but no one seemed to be interested in a motivational book with a country in such a depression with unemployment so high. He then moved to Chicago and took another job.

One day, he mentioned this manuscript to a friend of his who happened to know a publisher. *Pushing to the Front* was subsequently published and became a runaway bestseller in the nation. It was acclaimed by the leading business people in America as being the book that brought America into the twentieth century, thereby exerting an impact on the minds of decision-makers in the country. People like Henry Ford, Thomas Alva Edison, Harvey Firestone, and J.P. Morgan all read this book and were inspired by it.

As a way of "passing it on," Orison Swett Marden reported that, "There are two essential requirements for success. The first is 'get-to-itiveness,' and the second is 'stick-to-itiveness.' For him, there is no failure for a person who gets up every time they fall, who rebounds like a rubber ball, who persists when everyone else gives up, who pushes when everyone else turns back. Don't give up when you are on the verge of success, at the last minute of the game, or one foot away from a winning touchdown.

This poem "Don't Quit," written by an anonymous author, could help when you are tempted to quit or stop trying:

> When things go wrong; as they sometimes will.
> When the road you're trudging seems all uphill.
> When the funds are low, and the debts are high.
> And you want to smile, but you have to sigh.
>
> When care is pressing you down a bit.
> Rest, if you must, but don't you quit.
> Life is queer with its twists and turns.
> As every one of us sometimes learns.

And many a failure turns about;
When he might have won had he struck it out:
Don't give up though the pace seems slow,
You may succeed with another blow.

Success is failure turned inside-out;
The silver tint of the clouds of doubt
And you never can tell how close you're.
It may be near when it seems so far.

So, stick to the fight when you're hardest hit;
It's when things seem worst that you mustn't QUIT.

Alone with the Infinite Intelligence, the Power of Prayer

Great men are men of prayer. Some time ago, I went to visit one of my success mentors (Emeka Onwumere of blessed memory) in his resident compound. On arrival, I was a bit dumbfounded and surprised to see such a dignified person praying the Holy Rosary – a Roman Catholic praying method. He likened praying to the Creator as the interaction between the branches of a tree to its root. It reminded me of what Jesus Christ says,

> "I'm the true vine, and my Father is the vine dresser; every branch that does bear fruit he prunes to make it bear even more . . . I'm the vine, you're the branches. Whoever remains in me, and me in him bears fruit in plenty; for cut off from me you can do nothing. Anyone who doesn't remain in me is like a branch that has been thrown away – he withers" (Jn. 15:1-2; 5-6).

I grew up in a family where prayer (communicating with the Creator) was taken seriously. My parents, immediately after dinner, would call us together in the living room for the family prayer. First, some hymnals were intoned by anybody and afterwards came the prayer. We had the Bible reading, sharing and reflection, which implanted in us the spirit of togetherness and living the life of "*arête*" (the life of virtue). Through this means, we were made to understand the need and necessity of communion with the Creator. This not only brought peace of mind but has continued to bring internal power and happiness to me.

Norman Vincent Peale (in *The Power of Positive Thinking*) tells of the enormous impact of prayer in the lives of individuals. In his own view, prayer:

- Generates a peaceful mind.
- Draws in constant energy.
- Solves personal problems.
- Embodies healing virtues.
- Empowers.

One day, a friend asked another: "How is it that you're always so happy? You have so much energy, and you never seem to get down."

With her eyes smiling, she said: "I know the secret!"

"What secret is that?"

She replied: "I'll tell you all about it, but you have got to promise to share the secret with others. The secret is this: I have learned there is little I can do in my life that will make me truly happy. I must depend on God to make me happy and to meet my needs. When a need arises in me, I have to trust God to supply according to His riches. I have learned that most of the time I do not need half of what I think I do. He has never let me down. Since I learned that secret, I'm happy."

You might think that to be simple. But upon reflecting over her own life, she recalled how she thought a bigger house would make her happy, but it didn't. She thought a better-paying job would make her happy, but it didn't. When did she realize her greatest happiness? Sitting on the floor with her grandchildren, playing games, eating pizza, or reading a story. A simple gift from God.

Now you know it too! We cannot depend on people to make us happy. Only the Creator, in his infinite wisdom, can do that. Trust Him completely. And now that I have passed the secret on to you, what will you do? You've got to tell someone the secret too!

On turning open the pages of the Bible, one will not fail to discover where we are admonished to connect with the Creator. For instance, Jesus

Christ says, "We ought always to pray and not to lose heart" (Lk.18:1). It was of scriptural record that Daniel prayed not less than three times in a day. The Bible says, "When Daniel heard that the document had been signed, he retired to his house. The windows of his upstairs room faced toward Jerusalem. Three times each day he continued to fall on his knees, praying and giving praise to God as he had always done" (Dan. 6:11). This singular act of prayer also applied to other men like Elijah, Elisha, Job, Esther, and Judith.

Prayer generates a peaceful mind. There are practical ways by which you can develop serenity and quiet attitudes; one of them is your conversation. Depending on the words we use and the tone in which we use them, we can talk ourselves into being nervous, high-strung, and upset. Also, through our speech we can achieve quiet reactions: talk peacefully to be peaceful. Another effective technique in developing a peaceful mind is the daily practice of silence. For Norman Vincent Peale, everyone should insist upon not less than a quarter of an hour of absolute quiet every twenty-four hours. To Thomas Carlyle, "Silence is the element in which great things fashion themselves."

Go alone into the quietest place available to you and sit or lie down for fifteen minutes and practice the art of silence. Don't talk to anyone, don't write, don't read, think as little as possible, throw your mind into neutrality, and conceive your mind as a quiescent, inactive. Although this won't be easy at first because thoughts are stirring up in your mind, practice will increase your efficiency. When you've attained a quiescent state, then begin to listen for the deeper sounds of harmony and the beauty of God that are to be found in the essence of silence. The book of the Prophet Isaiah says, "But they that wait upon the Lord shall renew their strength; they shall mount up with wings as eagles; they shall run and not be weary, and they shall walk and not faint" (Is. 40:31).

Contact with God establishes within us a flow of the same type of energy that re-creates the world and that renews springtime every year. When in spiritual contact with God, said Norman Vincent Peale, through our thought processes, the divine energy flows through the personality and automatically renews the original creative act. Ponder on what happened to the apostles on the day of Pentecost (Acts 2:1-4).

When divine contact is broken, the personality gradually becomes depleted in body, mind, and spirit. As an electronic clock connected with an outlet doesn't run down and will continue indefinitely to keep accurate time, so is the body connected to the divine. Unplug the electronic clock and it stops; so it is with the body. To Knute Rockne (a one-time American football coach), "a football player can't have sufficient energy unless his emotions are under spiritual control."

One day (as told by Norman Vincent Peale), Walter Huston, the actor, sat by Jack Smith's desk. He noted a big sign on the wall on which were penciled the following letters: APRPBWPRAA. Surprised, Huston asked, "What do these letters mean?" Smith laughed and said, "They stand for **Affirmative Prayers Release Powers By Which Positive Results Are Accomplished**."

Great people apply these formulas to connect and draw on the spiritual energy:

1. Prayerize
2. Picturize
3. Actualize

By "prayerize," I mean a daily system of creative prayer. By picturize, I emphasize that those who assume success tend already to have success, while those who assume failure tend to have failure. When you prayerize and picturize, you will be astonished at how the picture actualizes.

Takeaway from Chapter Nine

- ▶ Rome wasn't built in a single day; so, also, is success. The journey of a thousand miles begins with a step. The number-one rule of the game of success is perseverance. Now is not the right time to quit. If you're tired, maybe take a rest, but don't quit!

- ▶ Whatever you want is right out of your comfort zone. What separates achievers from failures is that achievers continue where and when the quitters stop.

- ▶ Take your time to interact with any well-known achiever near you to hear their success principles.

- ▶ If you think you have tried enough, remember Thomas Alva Edison, who failed up to 10,000 times. Those are not failures but ways that did not work.

- ▶ "Cut off from me, you can do nothing," says Jesus Christ. To achieve more, align yourself with the Creator; for in Him we live and have our being.

CHAPTER TEN

Don't Lock Horns, Lock Hands

"Pay any price to stay in the presence of extraordinary people."
—Mike Murdock

Common Sense isn't Common

Oftentimes I have heard the mantra that "common sense isn't common," but I failed to understand it until I came across a passage in the scripture about a time Jesus Christ had gone into the temple and was teaching when the chief priests and the elders came to him and said, "What authority do you have for acting like this? And who gave you this authority?"

"And I," replied Jesus, "will ask you a question, just one; if you tell me the answer to it, I will then tell you my authority of acting like this. John's baptism: where did it come from: heaven or man?" The chief priests were taken by surprise, "And they argued it out this way among themselves; if we say from heaven, he will retort, then why did you refuse to believe him? But if we say from man, we have the people to fear, for they all hold that John was a prophet. So, their reply to Jesus was, we don't know. And he retorted, nor will I tell you my authority for acting like this" (Matt. 21:23-27; Mk.11:27-33).

As you aspire to rise to the top, there are certain skills and techniques you need to clothe yourself with. There are certain tactics you need to acquire: the need for a tough mind and tender heart. If Jesus Christ were still on earth, he would like to add, "Be ye therefore wise as serpents, and harmless as doves" (Matt.10:16).

In the light of Martin Luther King, Jr., it's pretty difficult to imagine a single person having both the characteristics of the serpent and the dove (although that's what Jesus expects). Considering the characteristics of tough-minded individuals, Martin Luther explains that:

- The tough mind is sharp and penetrating, breaking through the crust of legends and myths and sifting the true from the false.

- The tough-minded individual is astute and discerning. He has a strong, austere quality that makes for firmness of purpose and solidness of commitment.

- Soft-minded individuals are prone to embrace all kinds of superstitions; their minds are constantly invaded by irrational fears.

- The soft-minded person always fears change; he feels security in the status quo and has an almost morbid fear of the new.

- The hard-hearted person never truly loves; never experiences the beauty of friendship (because he's too cold to feel affection for another and too self-centered to share another's joy and sorrow).

- The hard-hearted person lacks the capacity for genuine compassion; unmoved by the pains and afflictions of his fellow human beings.

Here's a technique you should be aware of in your journeying to "Unknown Island":

- Be diplomatic

Some time ago, I was exchanging ideas with one of my good school friends, Charles, who expressed that telling people what they would like to hear is being diplomatic. In other words, don't tell people the whole "truth," and don't tell them what they aren't supposed to hear.

Is this diplomacy? Being diplomatic is more than that. The Nigerian author McDon, shedding some light on the concept of diplomacy, says life is like a game of football, whereby for you to be victorious, you must recognize that it is a game, know how to play it, know the rules governing it, be willing to obey the rules, and know how to manipulate the rules sometimes to suit your purpose.

I am in awe of Jesus Christ, and I hold Him in high esteem. His high sense of diplomacy fascinates me, especially in His encounter with the Pharisees and Sadducees (including the chief priests and elders) while still on earth; that is why I ascribe to Him as being all things to all men. There are several instances in the Bible to support that.

The scriptural narrative goes thus:

> . . . then the Pharisees (people of the Jewish religious sect who held strict obedience to the Torah, combined with traditional interpretations of it) went away to work out between them how to trap him in what he said, and they sent their disciple to him together with the Herodians to say, "Master, we know that you're an honest man who teaches the way of God in an honest way, and that you aren't afraid of anyone because a man's rank means nothing to you. Tell us your opinion, then is it permissible to pay taxes to Caesar or not?" But Jesus was aware of their malice and replied, "You hypocrites, why do you set this trap for me? Let me see the money you pay the tax with"; They handed him a denarius, and he said, "Whose head is this, whose name?" "Caesar's," they replied. He then said to them, "Very well, give back to Caesar what belongs to Caesar, and to God what belongs to God. This reply took them by surprise, and they left him alone and went away (Matt. 22:15-22).

Throughout the period of His existence on earth, He often spoke in parables, leaving no chance for the Pharisees to really figure out His statement or implicate Him by it. He always gave them a point to ponder any time He met with them. No wonder that, trying to give an answer to the question asked by His disciples on why He talked to them in parables, He said, "The reason I talk to them in parables is that they look without seeing and listen without hearing or understanding" (Matt.13:10-14). He always made statements that were subject to varying interpretations, hence making the Pharisees dig their own grave with their interpretations.

McDon was of the view that to be diplomatic is to learn and master the art of fantasy. We live in a world where people are never comfortable with naked truth. A world where people appreciate fantasies; hence, to pass any message to them you must be ready to conceal it in the midst of fantasies. Naked truth creates enmity for you. Thus, to be diplomatic is not to tell the truth; rather, it's the ability to tell the truth in a subtle way. This doesn't suggest that you don't tell the truth but tell people the truth with courtesy.

The best way to create enemies for yourself is to tell the naked truth, which hurts. When you say to someone, "You're a fool," the person in question may feel very offended but when you say, "People may see you as one who is unreasonable based on the way you do things or live your life," the person may feel less offended, although both convey the same message. The second one is an indirect way of saying someone is a fool (though it is appealing to the ear); it is diplomatic in nature. The more you hurt people, the more you create obstacles for yourself on your way to the top. To rise to the top, you have to avoid the naked truth. Don't join the mediocre who rush to tell the naked truth as did the soldier who, in his quest to tell David the naked truth about Saul and Jonathan's death, met his own death (2 Sam.1:1-16).

Work with People, Avoid Clowns

These could be the most important words in your life: You can't do a good deal with a bad partner. In the opinion of Lee Iacocca, "In the end, all business operations can be reduced to three words: people, product, and profit. Unless you've got a good team, you cannot do much with the other two." Have a critical panorama around you; whenever you have a struggling business, a bad marriage, or an investment gone bad, the pointing finger should go to the bad partner. This doesn't mean that the person is bad, but that you have the wrong partnership or teammates.

It is against this background that the rich dad, after his encounter with Robert T. Kiyosaki (as stipulated in the *Midas Touch*), who experienced business failures, was of the view that "it is simple, because he has partnership with the wrong people – these people he called clowns." Having the wrong or right partner presents many benefits or dangers:

- You cannot do a good deal with a bad partner.
- You get offered a lot of good deals when you're a good partner.
- From bad deals come good partners.
- Good people can make bad partners.
- Inexperienced good people don't get invited into the best deals.

Countless books have emphasized the need for building a lasting relationship in our daily life endeavors, especially as you aspire to climb to the top of the ladder of success. For instance, Brian Tracy (in *The Psychology of Selling*) was of the view that prospects will buy from you whenever they recognize that you're offering something to them. He called this "friendship factor." The South African/Australian business tycoon Brian Sher, in his book *What Rich People Know and Desperately Want to Keep Secret*, talked of four competitive advantages. One of them is of primary concern here: your people. In his view, your people are your greatest asset – not your brand, equipment, or products. They're the ones who make your products or services, find your customers, sell to them, and do everything else that makes your business a business.

Relationships say a lot as you aspire to greatness in life, be it in business, sports, academics, or music. Building a strong relationship gives fulfillment. John C. Maxwell, in *Today Matters*, highlights some fundamental elements as to why relationships matter:

1. Life's greatest experiences involve other people.
2. You will enjoy life more if you like people.
3. You will get farther in life if people like you.
4. People are any organization's most appreciable asset.

There is an old saying in sales: all things being equal, the likeable person wins. But all things not being equal, the likeable person still wins. Consultant John Luther opines that, "Natural talent, intelligence and a wonderful education do not guarantee success but the sensitivity to understand what other people want and the willingness to give it to them. Thus, worldly success depends on pleasing others."

My success principle anchors on working as a **TEAM – Together Each Achieve More**. For Sydney Newton Bremer, the simple definition of team-work is "coordination of effort." This is a fundamental principle of success, for all who would rise above mediocrity need the assistance and efforts of others. The life of the honeybee demonstrates a remarkable example of cooperation. Each hive contains workers, a queen, and drones. Each of these have assigned duties, which are executed with a never-failing distribution of labor and precision. The queen even has her own court, which consists of ten to fifteen workers who always form a circle around her and face her. While she lays eggs, they feed her and attend to her needs. During times when she is not laying eggs, they stroke her body, encouraging her to lay more eggs.

Queen bees are fully reproductive females who lay eggs in order to perpetuate the colony. The drones are the males, and their only function is to mate with the queens. They are not "put up" for the winter; instead, they're put to death by the workers or run off. The thousands of workers are underdeveloped females who gather food, care for the young, and keep the hive in order. Some serve as guards, air-conditioners, cell builders, repair crews, and many other cooperative tasks that go into keeping each colony in model housekeeping order.

So, in this analogy, cooperative effort could entail:

- The cooperation between people who group themselves together or form alliances for the purpose of attaining a given end under the principles known as the Law of the Mastermind (already discussed).

- The cooperation between the conscious and the subconscious minds, which form a reasonable hypothesis of man's ability to contact, communicate with, and draw upon "infinite intelligence."

Cooperation is all around us. Since we are living in an age of cooperative effort, nearly all successful businesses are conducted under this form of cooperation. Let's consider a few of them.

- Doctors and lawyers have their alliances for mutual aid and protection in the form of bar associations and medical associations.

- Bankers have both local and natural associations for their mutual aid and advancement.

- Retail merchants have associations for the same purpose.

- Automobile owners have grouped themselves into clubs and associations.

- Printers, plumbers, and coal dealers have associations.

- Nations have their cooperative alliances.

If all these have their cooperative alliances, which serves as part of their success, why can't you? So, ask yourself: who is my partner? Who am I locking hands with as I aspire to get to the top? Always bear in mind the words of Napoleon Hill: "Success in life can't be attained except through peaceful, harmonious, cooperative effort; nor can success be attained single-handedly or independently."

This suggests that success is not just a result of individual efforts, but also relies significantly on working effectively with others. Cooperation and teamwork are essential, and building positive, supportive relationships with others can enhance one's ability to succeed. Consider the success of a tech startup. While the founder might have the initial idea and vision, turning this concept into a successful business requires a diverse team. Engineers, marketers, salespeople, and support staff must all work together harmoniously and cooperatively. Each team member contributes unique skills and ideas, and their collaborative effort is crucial for developing the product, refining the business strategy, and engaging customers effectively.

Takeaway from Chapter Ten

▶ From the outset, it is popularly held and believed that common sense isn't common. How have you been able to convey your message to others without hurting their feelings?

▶ Virtue lies in the middle. In your success process, you need to have a soft mind and a tender heart.

▶ People want the "truth," but not the naked truth. Be all things to all people.

▶ As a business cannot function with bad partners, you cannot soar with eagles by chuckling with the turkeys. In your success process, differentiate between "clowns" and good partners.

▶ Success is people, people are success. People are ready to help you. But then, are you ready to satisfy their needs?

CHAPTER ELEVEN

You've Got Lemons, Make Lemonade

"Do not take life too seriously. You will never get out of it alive. If you have lemons, make lemonade."

—Elbert Hubbard

Doing Stupid Things is Just Part of the Game:

Sometime ago, Rev. Fr. Eugene Azorji, during one of his sermons, talked about what he called the "foolish things I have done." He talked about one faulty thing he did when he was a teenager. He concluded by saying, "It's just part of life; it's part of the game." If and when you say that something is just part of life or the game, you are simply telling someone not to be surprised or upset by something even when there are problems.

To make a juxtaposition between Simon Peter and Judas Iscariot, what is the primordial difference existing between these personalities? Can you recall the different acts performed by them? Judas Iscariot betrayed Jesus while Simon Peter (the head of the twelve apostles) denied Jesus three times. But nobody wants to go by the name Judas Iscariot, while others are taking up the name Peter. The truth is that Peter asked for forgiveness after the denials (Matt .26:69-75; Mk.14:66-72); while Judas didn't; rather, he went and hanged himself (Matt. 27:3-5).

What makes our life 100%? Is it money? No! Leadership? No!

Every problem has a solution if we just change our attitude.

Attitude? Yes! It helps to define a person, as in these examples:

- Although an individual can achieve success without a good attitude, their attitude will determine how much they enjoy the success.
- Your attitude at the beginning of a task affects its outcome more than anything else.
- Your attitude toward others often determines their attitude toward you.
- Your attitude can give you a winner's perspective.
- Your attitude – not your achievements – gives you happiness.
- Your attitude is contagious; you cannot have a bad attitude and encourage others at the same time. Conduct yourself like the person you want to become.

Your attitude determines your altitude and the level of your achievements. Research on the "cycle of completion" (a theory developed by Jack Canfield) says there are about five steps in completing a task or executing an idea.

In each of these steps – Decide, Plan, Start, Continue, and Finish, it's your attitude that matters most. It is really unfortunate that some people, after completing these steps, never finish.

The number-one key factor found in the lives of people who go from deciding to completion is their attitude. Those who stop or quit on the way we call failures or quitters; others who complete the cycle, we call the achievers.

Research says that failing to complete robs you of valuable units. In my own struggle to move out of the camp of mediocrity, there were certain times when what I had decided on couldn't get to completion until I discovered the secret.

So why don't people complete tasks? Sometimes this come from simply not having adequate systems, knowledge, or expertise for handling tasks. Other times it's because of bad work habits. Always ask yourself: what does it take to actually get this task or project completed?

David Allen developed a formula called **The Four D's of Completion**: Do it, Delegate it, Delay it, or Dump it. It is a time-management principle that helps individuals manage their tasks and responsibilities more effectively by categorizing them into actionable steps. Taking it into practice, when you pick up a piece of paper, decide then and there whether you will ever do anything with it, and if not, dump it. If you can take care of it within ten minutes, do it immediately. If you still want to take care of it yourself, but now it will take longer, delay it by filing it in a folder of things to do later. If you cannot do it yourself or do not want to take the time, delegate it to someone you trust to accomplish the task, but be sure to have the person report back when he/she finishes it so you know it is complete.

Having learned this, turn a minus into a plus. Dale Carnegie (*How to Stop Worrying and Start Living*) told of his encounter with Robert Maynard Hutchins (chancellor of the University of Chicago). In asking Hutchins how he conquered worry, the reply was that when you have a lemon, make lemonade. The fool, if he finds that life has handed him a lemon, gives up and says: "I'm beaten; it is fate, and I haven't got a chance," thereby indulging in an orgy of self-pity. But if the wise person is handed a lemon, he says, "What lesson can I learn from this misfortune? How can I improve my situation? How can I turn this lemon into lemonade?"

Two men looked out from prison bars. One saw the mud, the other saw the stars. Though the best things are the most difficult, always look for the stars. Supporting you in your path to make lemonade out of lemon, Douglas Malloch advises a person to embrace and excel in whatever position or situation they find themselves, even if it's not the most prestigious or glamorous. Whether you're a humble scrub in the valley instead of a majestic pine on a hill, or a small bass instead of a large muskie, what matters is that you strive to be the best in that role. Ultimately, your success and fulfillment come from how well you perform your role, regardless of its size or visibility. In trying to make lemonade out of lemons, get concerned about your attitude, which gives you possibilities.

Use Feedback to Your Advantage

Yes! Feedback is everywhere. For instance, we have it in the academic sphere, in music, sports, and the software development environment. It is also in the scripture. In the reconnaissance in Canaan (Num.13:1-13),

Joshua's spies on Jericho and the spies return (Jos. 2:1-24) and the counting made by the seventy-two disciples who were sent out by Jesus Christ (Lk. 10:1-20) all had feedback.

In your aspiration to the top of the ladder of success, always remember to walk and work with feedback. Ken Blandhard and Spencer John (coauthors of *The One Minute Manager*) say that "feedback is the breakfast of champions." Once you begin to act, you will start getting feedback about whether you are doing the "commonly" right thing or not; because to some people, for you to get along, you must go along. People will be there to impress their own definition of success on you, to suggest to you what to do and give you advice and directives. Once you have started receiving feedback (talking more to yourself and less to others), take it to heart and start working on it.

There are two kinds of feedback– negative and positive. The positive serves as money, praise, raise, and promotion. The negative serves as critique. There's no doubt that we may prefer the positive to the negative. To reach your goals quickly, you need to welcome, receive, and embrace all the feedback that comes your way. After all, as Buckminster Fuller says, "Human beings were given a left foot and a right foot to make a mistake first to the left, then to the right, left again and repeat."

However, from research, there are ways of responding to feedback that don't work, including:

- Caving in and quitting
- Getting mad at the source of the feedback
- Ignoring the feedback

Be willing to ask for feedback from friends, family, business partners, loved ones, relatives, and supervisors because you're better off knowing the truth than not knowing the truth at all. When you receive feedback, acknowledge it and thank the person for their input, support, or suggestions. Listen to it and absorb it with a level head; probe into what they have said and decide whether it is valid, relevant, and useful for your improvement. Be honest about your strengths and weaknesses. Is all feedback accurate? No, because some is polluted by either bias or the psychological distortions of the person giving you feedback. Things you may like to do when you have received feedback include:

- Acknowledge you did the best with the knowledge you had at that time.
- Acknowledge that you can cope with any of the consequences and results.
- Write down everything you have learned from the experience.
- Make sure to thank everyone for their feedback and insights.
- Take some time to go back and review your successes.
- Regroup.
- Refocus on your vision.

John Mason, in *Imitation is Limitation*, said every great idea has these possible responses:

1. It's impossible – don't waste time and energy
2. It's possible but has a limited value
3. I said all along it was a good idea.

If your head sticks up above the crowd, expect more criticism than applause. Those who can, do, while those who can't, criticize. Always remember that sticks and stones are only thrown at fruit-bearing trees. If it weren't for the doers the critics would soon be out of business. Ride on!

Takeaway from Chapter Eleven

▸ To succeed in life is to know the rules and play by them. At one time you may have done some foolish things. You have to say: "Well, it's just part of life; it's part of the game."

▸ What is it that makes your life 100%? Is it money? Love? Luck? Is it leadership? The answer is simply your ATTITUDE.

▸ What separates achievers from failures is that achievers decide on their goals, tasks, and project and take it to the completion phase, while the latter quit on the way.

▸ There's a secret guide to success: critique. Hear more, say less.

▸ When people criticize you, it really says something on your part (and that of the person offering the critique). On your part, it shows that you can do while on their part, they know the way but can't drive the car.

CHAPTER TWELVE

Success Tomorrow is Today's Preparatory Action

"Things may come to those who wait,
but only the things left by those who hustle."

—Abraham Lincoln

Take Charge and Control of the Fisherman's Bait

Opportunity comes once. A story was told about a king who had a boulder placed in the middle of a roadway. Then he hid himself and watched to see if anyone would remove the huge block. Some of the king's wealthiest merchants and courtiers came by and simply walked around it. Many loudly blamed the king for not keeping the roads clear, but none did anything about getting the stone out of the way.

Then, a peasant came along carrying a load of vegetables. Upon approaching the boulder, he laid down his burden and tried to move the stone to the side of the road. After much pushing and straining, he finally succeeded. After, the peasant picked up his load of vegetables and he noticed a purse lying on the road where the boulder had been. Fortunately, the purse contained many gold coins and a note from the king indicating that the gold was for the person who removed the boulder from the roadway.

Every opportunity is a chance to improve our successes. Thus, always stay in the environment that offers you that opportunity. Never rush at opportunities – be mindful of what is offered for free!

Robert Greene (in *48 Laws of Power*) was of the view that what is offered for free is dangerous – it usually involves either a trick or a hidden obligation. What has value is worth paying for. By paying your own way, you stay clear of gratitude, guilt, and deceit. It is also often wise to pay the full price, for there are no cutting corners with excellence. When friends, for instance, offer you something for free, you can be sure they expect something in return and they are making you feel indebted; he who receives freely is a debtor. The powerful never forget that whatever is offered for free is inevitably a trick. Why don't you join the group of the powerful?

When fishermen go to the sea to fish, they pray to the gods and goddesses of the sea to send them what's called "jolly-fish." This is because this kind of fish never sees beyond what it intends to eat; it never takes time to reflect on the bait from the fisherman that is dangling; rather, it will joyfully rush for its food and in the process is caught and trapped by the hook of the fisherman. This isn't the same with the wise fish. It never sees a worm in the sea and rushes at it. First, it takes its time to go round the bait, moving upward, downward, and in different directions until it is sure.

People have witnessed a success crash because they were once like the jolly-fish. Thus, as you get ready to take your first parachute jump, keep in mind this Japanese saying: "Nothing is more costly than something given free of charge." Always go over, around, and behind and think over it!

Act As If; Do It Now

The world does not pay you for what you know; rather, it pays you for what you can do with what you know. In other words, the universe rewards action. In giving a summary of failure and success, one thing comes to mind – ACTION. Winners act. To be successful, you've got to do what successful people do, and successful people are highly action-oriented. Know that nothing happens until you act.

Think of the example I used earlier of Jack Canfield and the $100 bill; this demonstrates the importance of taking action. This is exactly what you need to do to succeed in life after reading and digesting the principles in this book. If your ship does not come in, swim out to meet it; do not wait around for fate. Take action to achieve your goals.

There is no perfect time to start. It is time for you to quit waiting for:

- Perfection
- Inspiration
- Permission
- Reassurance
- The right person to come along
- Someone to discover you
- More self-confidence
- And a clear instructions/principles

Get into action. Stop aiming and getting ready. Just keep firing and keep readjusting. Remember that the last six letters in the word "satisfaction" are ACTION. To get satisfied, get into action, now. As you get ready, always remember to **ACT AS IF**. Act as if you're already where you want to be, as this programs the RAS – Reticular Activating System. Don't be afraid of mistakes because they're just opportunities for learning something new. I recommend you adopt the formula/principle of DIN – Do It Now. Ray Bradbury (prolific American author) said "First you jump off the cliff, and you build wings on the way down."

Takeaway from Chapter Twelve

▶ Action, they say, speak louder than words. What separates high achievers from failures is simply ACTION.

▶ Wach out for gifts that are offered free (just like the wise fish) as you aspire to the top of the ladder. If possible, go round, over, or behind them.

▶ Opportunities are rare and typically present themselves only once. You should act quickly and decisively when they arise. Even so, never be in a rush for opportunity.

▶ For satisfACTION, get into ACTION

Meet You at the Top!

Bibliography

Lorimer T. Lawrence & Lechner Doris E. (1994): *The New Webster's Dictionary of the English Language*; Lexicon Publications, Inc., United States of America.

Hornby A. S. (2000): *Oxford Advanced Learner's Dictionary of Current English* (6th ed.); Oxford University Press, New York, United States of America.

Coventry Lucinda & Nixon Martin (1999): *The Oxford English Minidictionary* (5th ed.); Oxford University Press, New York, United States of America.

Jones Alexander (1974): *The Jerusalem Bible* (popular ed.); Darton, Layman & Todd Ltd., and Doubleday & Company, Inc. 89 Lillie Road, London.

Allen James (2010): *Mind is the Master* (The Complete James Allen Treasury); Jeremy P. Torcher/Penguin Group, Inc., New York, U.S.A.

Hill Napoleon (1928): *The Law of Success*; Jeremy P. Torhcer/Penguin Group Inc., New York, U.S.A.

Hill Napoleon & Stone Clement W. (1960): *Success Through a Positive Mental Attitude*; Pocket Books Inc., New York, U.S.A.

Hill Napoleon (2003): *Think and Grow Rich*; Vermilion Publishing Inc., London.

Greene Robert (2000): *The 48 Laws of Power*; Penguin Group Inc., New York, U.S.A.

Tracy Brian (2004): *Goals (How to Get Everything You Want – Faster Than You Ever Thought Possible)*; Berrelt-Kochler Publishers, Inc., San Francisco, U.S.A.

Tracy Brian (2004): *The Psychology of Selling (Increase Your Sales Faster and Easier Than You Thought Possible)*; Nelson Business Publishers, Inc., United States of America.

Canfield Jack (2007): *How to Get from Where You Are to Where You Want to Be*; HarperCollins Publishers Ltd., U.S.A.

Letchter Sharon & Reid Greg (2011): *Three Feet from Gold*; Jaico Publishing House, Mumbai, India.

Devaraj S. (2012): *Dare to Fail You'll Excel*; Published by Better Yourself Books, Mumbai, India.

Frank Prabbal (2009): *People Manipulation* (Second Rev. ed.); Sterling Publishers Ltd., New Delhi.

Francis Xavier G. (2004): *The World's Most Inspiring Thoughts for Self-Improvement*; Think Achieve Prosper Publications, Bangalore, India.

Bremer Newton Sydney (1996): *How to Get What You Want*; Published in Nigeria by Rhema Publishing Ministry Inc.

Jesumani Antonette (2009): *A to Z tips for Success*; Published by Pauline Sisters Bombay Society, Mumbai, India.

Deep Sam & Lyle Sussman (1996): *Yes, You Can!* Published by True Life Christian Publications, Benin City, Edo State, Nigeria.

Martin Luther King, Jr. (1987): *Strength to Love*; Fortress Press, Philadelphia, U.S.A.

Mason John (2009): *Imitation is Limitation*; Published by Orient Paperbacks, New Delhi, India.

Allen Robert G. (2005): *Multiple Streams of Income (How to Generate a Lifetime of Unlimited Wealth!)*; Published by John Wiley & Sons, Inc., Hoboken, New Jersey, U.S.A.

D'Sousa Charles S. (2010): *Keys to Success in Life* (3rd print); Published by Better Yourself Books, Mumbai, India.

Kapena Sumbye (2007): *You Can Succeed* (3rd print); Published by Better Yourself Books, Mumbai, India.

Schuller Robert H. (1988): *Tough Times Never Last, But Tough People Do!* Published by Orient Paperbacks, New Delhi, India.

Kenny Cedric M. (2009): *Study Smart Score High (An Innovative guide to Learning effectively and staying ahead)*; Printed and Published by Sterling Publishers Prt. Ltd., New Delhi, India.

Bragdon Allen D. & Gamon David (2005): *Use it or Lose it (How to Keep Your Brain Fit as it Ages)*, (2nd print); Published by Better Yourself Books, Mumbai, India.

Schuller Robert H. (2010): *Be an Extraordinary Person in an Ordinary World*; Published by Orient Paperbacks, New Delhi, India.

Kiyosaki Robert T. & Lechter Sharon (2001): *Rich Dad Poor Dad*; Published by Warner Books, New York, U.S.A.

Kiyosaki Robert T. (2008): *Increase Your Financial IQ (Get Smarter With Your Money)*; Published by Business Plus, New York, U.S.A.

Carnegie Dale (1956): *How to Develop Self-Confidence & Influence People* by Public Speaking; Published by Pocket Books, New York, U.S.A.

Trump Donald J. & Kiyosaki Robert T. (2011): *Midas Touch (Why Some Entrepreneurs Get Rich and Why Most Don't)*; Published by Plata Plushing, U.S.A.

Clason George S. (1988): *The Richest Man in Babylon*; Published by Signet Book Inc., U.S.A.

Maxwell John C. (2004): *Today Matters*; Published by Center Street, New York, U.S.A.

Sukh Shammi (2010): *Managing Time*; Published by Better Yourself Books, Mumbai, India.

LaHaye Tim (1984): *Why You Act the Way You Do*; Published by Tyndale House Publishers, Inc., Wheaton, Illinois, U.S.A.

Collier Robert (2007): *The Secret of the Ages (The Master Code to Abundance and Achievement)*; Published by Jeremy P. Tarcher/Penguin Group Inc., New York, U.S.A.

Sharma Robin (2012): *The Leader Who Had No Title*; Published by Jaico Publishing House, Mumbai, India.

Atkinson Sue (2006): *Building Self-Esteem (A Practical Guide to Growing in Confidence)* (2nd print); Published by Better Yourself Books, Mumbai, India.

Allen James (2008): *As a Man Thinketh*; Published by the Pengium Group, New York, U.S.A.

Peale Vincent Norman: *The Power of Positive Thinking*; Published by Amaugo Christian Publication, Aba, Abia State, Nigeria.

Anthony Saji (2008): *40 Secrets for a Happy Life* (2nd print); Published by Better Yourself Books, Mumbai, India.

Scrampickal Jacob & Joseph Leela (2002): A TextBook for Media Education; Published by Better Yourself Books, Mumbai, India.

Sher Brian (2000): *What Rich People Know & Desperately Want to Keep Secret*; Nigerian edition, an imprint of Purpose-Driven Publishing Group, Benin City, Nigeria.

Oparaugo Barnabas (2010): *Empower Your WillPower (A Psycho-Philosophic Therapy to Your Under Challenged Or Wounded Self)*; Printed by Urekweson Press Ltd., Nigeria.

McDon Felix A. O. (2008): *You Can Rise to the Top*; Published by McDon Publishers, Nigeria.

Carson Ben (1992): *Think Big*; Published by Zondervan, U.S.A.

Index

80/20 rule
ABCDE method
Abigail
Abraham
Abraham Lincoln
Abram (later called Abraham)
Academia
Act as if
Actualize
Adamic fall
Adawai James
Admiral Robert Peary
Advance planning
Aesop
AFS – Achievers Focusing System
Agora
Agu Solomon
Albert Einstein
Albert Schweitzer
Alexander Graham Bell
Allen D. Bragdon
Allied force
Allied force (see also, Master Minders)
Alzheimer Disease (AD)
Amadi Henry
Andrew Carnegie
Anthony Robbins
Archbishop Fulton J. Sheen

Aristocrats

Aristotle

Arnold Schwarzenegger

Artisans

Ask

Attitude

Attractive personality (see also, pleasing personality)

Auguste

Autosuggestion

B. C. Forbes

Bank account

Barak Obama

Be original (also, unique)

Belief: head and heart

Ben Carson

Ben Stein

Benjamin Franklin

Biblical text (see also, scriptural content)

Bill Clinton

Bill Gates

Birthright

Bismarck Plan (see also, Plan B)

Blue-sky thinking

Brain: left, right, and subconscious mind

Breakdown for a breakthrough

Brin Sergey

Bruce Jenner

Buddha

Calvary

Canaanite woman

Cato

Cedric M. Kenny

Cell (weak and strong)

Chagrin

Charlatan

Charles Darwin

Charles M. Schwab

Chatters of voices

Cheap gold

Christ Jesus

Christopher Columbus

Chromosomes

Coach/teacher (see also, mentor)

Coma

Concentration

Confucius

Craftsmen

Creative procrastination

D.C.A. – Definite Chief Aim

Dale Carnegie

Dark Ages

Dasein

David Gamon

Declaration of Independence

Decryption (see, encryption)

Devic

DIN – Do It Now

Diplomacy

Disciples

Disciples

Discipleship

Disease germs

Dollar mark

Don Williams

Donald J. Trump

Dr. R. Buckminster Fuller

Dullard temperament: sanguine, choleric, melancholy, and phlegmatic

Dummy

Earl nightingale

Earnestness of purpose

Economic phase

Education

Egypt

Eidetic visualization

Ejike Mbaka (Rev. Fr.)

Elizabeth Kubler-Ross

Ella Wheeler Wilcox
Elvis A. Presley
Emershement
Emotional culprits
Empiricists (see also, rationalists)
Encryption (see, decryption)
Entrepreneur
Eugene Azorji (Rev. Fr. Dr.)
Eureka
Evolution
Examinations
Father (see also, dad)
Fear not (see also, don't worry)
Feedback
Felix McDon
Fiancé
Fiancée
Finance
Financial IQ
Francis Bacon
Franklin D. Roosevelt
Gabael
Galileo Galilei
Gens
George David
George F. Handel
George Washington Carver
Gloria Agwunobi
Goal book
Goal-setters
godfather (see also, mentorship, and role model)
Gold
Golden Age
Grand Masters
Greeks political arena
Guru
Habit
Haile Selassie

Heaven

Helen Adams Keller

Hell

Henry Brooke Adams

Henry Ford

Heredity: physical and social

Hitler

Holy Communion

Holy Rosary

Homer's Odyssey

Homo sapiens

Howard Gardener

Human creativity

Idi Amin

Idiota

Igbo tribe

IMAGE – Innovation Mastery Authenticity Guts and Ethics

Imagination (see also, visualization): reproductive and creative

Impostor

Index card (see also, journal)

Infinite Intelligence (see also, Christ Jesus)

Intelligences: verbal-linguistic, logical-mathematical, body-kinesthetic, spatial, musical, inter-personal, and intrapersonal

IPDE prescription

Iron Age

Isaac

J. N. Neipce

Jack Canfield

Jack Welch

Jacob

Jacob Riis

Jael

James Allen

Jean-Jacques Rousseau

Jet Li

Jim Rohn

John Assaraf

John C. Maxwell

John F. Kennedy

John Locke

John Logie Baird

John Mason

Joseph: the dreamer

Jotham's fable

Journal (see also, index card)

Judas Iscariot

Jude Onuoha (Rev. Fr. Dr.)

Julius Caesar

Junk

Knowledge: general and specialized

Knute Rockne

Kwame Nkrumah

L. J. M. Dauguerrre

Law of Attraction

Law of Belief

Law of Cause and Effect

Law of success

Law of the excluded alternative

Lightning calculators

Loss; of Love, Old age, Criticism, Poverty, Death

Louis Lumiere

Lukewarm people

LWT – Leader Without title

Lyle Sussman

Ma Bridget

Machiavelli

Magic-wand

Mankind

Manuscript

Marconi

Margaret Thatcher

Marie Curie

Mark Victor Hansen

Mark Zuckerberg

Martin Luther King

Martyrs

Masochists

Master Minders

Master Minders (see also, allied force)

Matthew's account

Mediocre (see also, idiota)

Meditation

Men of theoria

Mentality Change Organization

Mentor (see also, coach/teacher)

Mentorship (see also, god father)

Michael Ikegwuoha

Michael Jackson

Michael Jordan

Michelangelo

Midas Touch

Mike Murdock

Milo C. Jones

Mind mapping

Minds: scattered, shallow, and stable

Mindstorming

Minus sign

Mohammed Ali

Monks

Mother (see also, mum)

Mother Teresa

Mozart

Napoleon Bonaparte

Napoleon Hill

Nervous system: sympathetic, and voluntary or cerebrospinal

New Testament (OT)

NMA – Negative Mental Attitude

Noah Webster

Norman Vincent Peale

Nostra Demus

O.T. (Old Testament)

Oliver Wendell Holmes

On Purpose

OPM – Other Peoples' Money (see also, OPR)

OPR – Other Peoples' Resources (see also, OPM)
OPT (see also, OPM and OPR)
Orient
Orville Wright
Otto Van Bismarch
Owelle Rochas
Ozor Ernest
Paradigm shift
Pauper (see also, rich)
Pederasty
Pentecost
People manipulation
Percy Ross
Persistence
Personal computer (PC)
Philosopher-kings
Philosophy
Picturize
PIO – Pass It On
Plan B (see also, Bismarck Plan)
Plato
Pleasing Personality (see also, attractive personality)
Plus sign
PMA – Positive Mental Attitude
PMA – Positive Mental Attitude
Poor (see also, pauper, and wretched)
Positive expectation of yes
Prayer
Prayerize
Prediction
Pre-Socratics
Primates
Principle of causality
Principle of Justice
Procrastination
Prodigal son
Promised Land
Prophet Elijah

Prophet Elisha
Psychic phase
Psychologist
Quit (also, failed, stop)
R. U. Darby
Rahab
RAS – Reticular Activating System
Rationalists (see also, empiricists)
Reality Principle
Reason-why
Referee (Football) association
Rene Descartes
Reserve capacity
Rich (see also, well-to-do)
Richard Bach
Robert Collier
Robert G. Allen
Robert Greene
Robert H. Shuller
Robert T. Kiyosaki
Roman Catholic Church
Rosary
Rudyard Kipling
Ruth Stafford Peale
S. Devaraj
S. I. Hayakawa
Saint Paul
Sam Deep
Sammi Sukh
Sarai (later called Sarah)
Saving habit
Seat of Wisdom
Self-concept
Self-esteem (see also, self-image)
Self-help book
Self-image (see also, self-esteem)
Seminar
Seminary

Senior seminarian (see also, seminarian)

Sense of control

Sergei Yeframov

Shakers/movers of the world

Shallow minders

Sheol

Side tracks (see also, distractions)

Sigmund Freud

Sir Isaac Newton

Six dangerous enemies of man

Socrates

Soft minds

Solomon

Spending habit

Spinach

Spiritualists

Sporters

Stalin

Stan Dale

STD – Stupid Things Done

Stephen Njoku (Rev. Fr.)

Steve Jobs

Stone Age

Stop-loss

Strength of character

Strong (see also, rich)

Structural tension

Success equation: $[(P + T) \times A \times A] + F = $ Your Success

Sydney Newton Bremer

Tally

Tamar

Tawni O'Dell

TEAM – Together Each Achieve More

Tete-a-tete

Thales

The Four D's

The Power of Positive Thinking

Thomas Edison

Thomas Paine

Three "P" formula

Three-ring binder

Tim LaHaye

Time management

Tobias

Tobith

To-do list

Tony Buzan

Tough minds

Tower of Babel

Twins

United States of America (USA)

Untimely death

W. Clement Stone

Walter Huston

Weak (see also, pauper)

Wilbur Wright

William Wilberforce

Willis H. Carrier

Will-Power

Winston Churchill

Woman's Club

Worry (see also, fear)

Worry of: poverty, old age, ill health, criticism, loss of love of someone, and death

Worry-aholic

Yahweh

Zebedee's sons

Zero-based thinking

Zig Ziglar

Zusammensein

Acknowledgments

There are so many people to thank and to appreciate for their tremendous support in helping to make this book a reality. As a believer in God, I would like to appreciate the presence of the Holy Trinity: God the Father, God the Son, and God the Holy Spirit.

How does a person say "thank you" when there are so many people to thank? Many helped me turn the raw ore of my ideas into precious metal, while others helped get that precious metal out into the world. They helped me hone the rough edges of the material and make it more presentable. Thank you to my family – parents, siblings, relatives, and to all my friends for allowing me the time, accommodating me, providing, and furnishing me with information when I needed them. You're all wonderful!

Gratitude, they say, is the mother of all virtues, and ingratitude is the worst vice. It's on that note that I wish to say: I'm grateful to you all.

Yes, we did it!

About the Author

Born and raised in the small community of Owerre-Umudioka in Imo state, Nigeria. Johnbosco is the fourth of five children. From an early age, he developed a keen interest in academics, which laid the foundation for his extensive research and academic background.

He completed his first degree in Nigeria in 2014 and went on to earn two master's degree in both Canada and USA (2021 and 2022 respectively). His passion for writing led him to publish his first book, "Idea Is Money," in 2013 – a literary narrative that outlines strategies for personal success.

Between 2019 to 2020, Johnbosco hosted a radio talk show, "All The Facts" in the USA, where he shared insights and knowledge on various topics.

He is the founder of I Need Scrummaster Inc., a consulting firm specializing in project management, also offers courses in Scrum and project management. He has diverse professional experience in both the private and public sectors.

He enjoys a variety of activities like watching comedy shows, playing soccer, and makes time for workouts at the gym. His curiosity drives him to constantly research topics that intrigue him. His guiding mantra is "only the best is good enough," a principle that reflects his commitment to excellence in all his pursuits. He currently resides in the beautiful island of Victoria, BC.

Printed in the USA
CPSIA information can be obtained
at www.ICGtesting.com
JSHW021206201124
73943JS00002B/6